Beyond Politics:
Inspirational People Of Israel

Ronda Robinson

Mazo Publishers

Beyond Politics
ISBN: 978-1-936778-91-1

Copyright © 2011 by Ronda Robinson

To contact the author
or for information on group book orders, visit
www.israelbeyondpolitics.com

Published by:
Mazo Publishers

P.O. Box 10474
Jacksonville, FL 32247 USA
1-815-301-3559

P.O. Box 36084
Jerusalem 91360 Israel
054-7294-565

Website: www.mazopublishers.com
Email: cm@mazopublishers.com

Book production by
Prestige PrePress
prestige.prepress@gmail.com

To my parents, Alfred and Sandy Robinson, for everything.

Acknowledgments

It takes a village to raise a child, and it took a village to help bring this book into the world. I am very indebted to everyone who gave me their time, trust, advice and encouragement, including:

My "visions" buddies Dee Snyder and Melinda Kirkland, my mentor Paul Ashdown and other master's project committee members Gilya Schmidt and Rob Heller, my brother and sister-in-law Richard Robinson and Aileen O'Neill, photographer David Silverman, Jason Stern of blessed memory, Davina and Oded Davidson and family, Noga Miller, Rabbi Yehoshua Kahan, Rabbi Ilan Feldman, Wade Saye, Nina Rubin, Moishe Bear, and Rabbi Moshe and Chana Poupko and family.

I am deeply grateful to A.J. Robinson and Nicole Ellerine, Natalie Robinson, Ian and Carol Ratner, Stuart Peskin and Deva Hirsch, Mark and Sharon Moskowitz, and Jeff and Anita Stein for their faith and support.

Special thanks to Chaim Mazo and his staff.

Also special thanks to Myra Manning, Al Kaff, Tom Glaser, Alon Liel, Bill Aron, Lloyd Wolf, Tom McCarter, Karen Rubin, Linda Weaver, Neil Shulman, Darryl Moland, Benyamin Cohen, Judy Merlis, Ruby Grossblatt, Leslie Lowenstein, David Mitchell, Rachael Siegelman, Ben and Jacquie Hirsch, Liz Lieberman, Joy Goodman, Rita Williams, J.C. Love, Jim Wells and Ann Wilson.

Thank You, God, for the inspiration and the gift of writing, my "magic carpet" to anywhere and everywhere.

Contents

Acknowledgments   4
About The Author   6
Preface   7

Inspirational People Of Israel

Rena Quint   13
Clara Hammer   21
Sara Lanesman   27
Lior Sasson   33
Liora Tedgi   41
Sarah Nachshon   47
Hanoch Teller   55
Miri Flusser   63
Chana Bracha Siegelbaum   71
Faydra Shapiro   77
Moshe Basson   85
Lev Strinkovsky   91
Sam Greene   99
Joe & Marion Goodstein   105
Davina Davidson   113
Elchanan Davidson   119
Yisrael Avidor   125
Shlomo Molla   135

About The Photographer   144

About The Author

Ronda Robinson is an award-winning journalist in Atlanta who enjoys writing feature stories about people, Judaism, travel, and health, fitness and wellness. She began her career as a reporter for weekly and daily newspapers. Her credits as a freelance writer/editor include many national and international publications, such as American Profile, Hadassah, Jerusalem Post, Jerusalem Report, Travel & Leisure, USA Today and CNN.com. She earned a bachelor's

degree from Stephens College and a master's degree from the University of Tennessee, where she was a journalism instructor. Raised in Knoxville, Tennessee, she also has lived in Israel.

Preface

I have been searching for home all my life. I found it on my first trip to Israel in 1994. My soul immediately felt comfortable there. As Rabbi Judah Halevi, one of the greatest Hebrew poets of the Middle Ages, said, "Though I am in the West, my heart is in the East."

Rabbi Nachman of Bratslav, a great-grandson of the Baal Shem Tov, the father of the Hasidic movement, wrote, "Wherever I go, I am going towards Eretz Yisrael (the Land of Israel)."

What is it that makes Israel so special? For me, the answer is threefold. First, Israel is the Jewish homeland – literally the Promised Land. The Bible comes alive and takes on new meaning when seeing where momentous events actually unfolded. Second, God is palpable there. I remember studying at Hebrew University one summer and having a strong sense of how close God was, almost as if I could reach out and touch Him from my dormitory balcony in Jerusalem. I still have that feeling when I visit Israel. Third, I feel a connection with the people. I meet a lot of soulful Israelis, both native Sabras and immigrants, on my trips there, and gravitate toward them. Discussions often are peppered with talk about God, Torah, Jewish mysticism, global cultures ... not the average fare elsewhere.

I fell in love with Israel on my first trip, and on the second one started dreaming about this book. It was the summer of 1996, when I was learning in an intensive language program at Hebrew University. I had begun meeting real Israelis – beyond the professional guides one encounters on sightseeing tours – and found them to be warm, colorful characters. The country was filled with remarkable people. There would be no shortage of personalities to fill a book and sequels.

My first assignment as a freelance writer for the Jerusalem Post that summer was a feature on an idea I had pitched about Clara Hammer, fondly known as "The Chicken Lady of Jerusalem." She was in her 80s then, yet had a lively, timeless spark about her and was a lovely soul to be around. As a retiree, she started a fund that grew to feed hundreds of needy families a traditional chicken meal on the Jewish Sabbath. While she loved talking about the chicken fund to drum up new donors, Clara, who died at age 99 in 2010, also would entertain visitors with an impromptu song or joke. I never saw her without a smile on her face and kind words on her lips.

Upon returning to America, I noticed that ordinary, inspiring citizens like Clara didn't make headlines in the Western media. Instead, I observed how the media used or created polarized stereotypes in reporting the news from Israel. Semiotics is the study of signs and symbols to explore how they create meaning. It seemed that reporters used tanks, bus explosions, suicide bombers and security walls to convey the world of Israel, as if the country lacked anything worthy of relating to beyond those convenient freeze frames.

I felt frustrated by this portrayal. As a journalist always interested in people features above politics, I wanted to show the other side of Israel – beyond the stereotypical headlines. I am committed to presenting a side not usually seen in the Western press. What Israelis have built out of the desert since 1948 is amazing.

This book is designed to put a human face to Israel. Through narrative and photos, it relates the personal stories of Jewish Israelis living ordinary lives in extraordinary times. They dance at weddings, sing at synagogue, repair violins, play symphonies, help children with homework and work six-day weeks. They also fear that someone they love might not survive a mundane trip to the local pizza parlor, the mall or a discotheque.

How can they hold this tension of the opposites, living rich lives punctuated by uncertainty? What draws them and makes them stay in an emotionally and economically challenging society?

My intention is to make a complex land approachable by introducing some of the colorful personalities who inhabit it – people who stand for their dreams. I am committed to helping you know Israel as a nation of individuals rather than disasters and stereotypes. Their stories of courage, humor and love cannot help but touch and inspire you about what's possible to create in the world. This book is designed to capture a snapshot in time of their lives.

I found most of my subjects through the liberal use of referrals and a generous dose of intuition. They represent a mosaic of Jewish Israelis – secular, religious, kibbutznik, villager, Sabra, immigrant, American, Australian, Danish, Scottish, Iraqi, Indian and everything in between. They range from a Jerusalem chef who specializes in Biblical cooking and "Land of Israel" food to a Hevron-area grandmother who doesn't let anything stand in the way of the covenant God made with Abraham, Isaac and Jacob.

As a friend pointed out, they seem coincidentally to be kindred spirits of mine; they are mostly unconventional souls on an inner journey that makes their hearts sing. Even though I live in America, my soul calls Israel home and replenishes itself by visiting there regularly. I am grateful to live in a time when that miracle is possible.

Beyond Politics:
Inspirational People Of Israel

Rena Quint

Holocaust Survivor – Volunteer
Born 1935, Piotrkow, Poland

Rena Quint

Dancing, Singing For Jews Who Never Could

An upbeat Holocaust survivor: That's what I discovered when I visited Rena Quint at her lovely four-bedroom Jerusalem apartment the night before her granddaughter's wedding. I learned that Rena's cheerful demeanor was related neither to the upcoming joyous occasion nor to the cruise from which she had just returned. Rather, she makes a choice to face the world with grace – despite having suffered so much as a child in a Polish ghetto, slave labor camp and German concentration camp.

I wondered if the interview was cathartic for Rena. She insisted not. "I've got too many good things going on," she told me. "I think I do this because I can and because I should."

Rena volunteers as a docent and gives testimony at Yad Vashem, Israel's Holocaust Martyrs' and Heroes' Remembrance Authority, for the same reason. When we met, she was refining introductory remarks for a Kristallnacht (German pogroms known as "Night of Broken Glass") program the following week at the Jossi Berger Holocaust Study Center, where she had served as president for 22 years. The theme for the annual event was "What Was the Writing on the Wall?"

Estee Yaari, the foreign media liaison at Yad Vashem who had put me in touch with Rena, called her an amazing, vibrant Holocaust survivor. I could see why.

After talking, drinking tea and eating cake with Rena for two hours, I felt surprisingly uplifted by this woman who would have every right to feel bitter about her past.

Instead, this is Rena's philosophy:

"I have a feeling we have to laugh for all those Jews who never had a chance to laugh. Dance for all those Jews who never had a chance to dance. Sing for all those Jews who never had a chance to sing. Live life to its fullest and be Jews they never had a chance to be. And thank God, we have a country where we have the possibility of doing that."

Motherless daughters often are good at mining coal for diamonds. Having survived the deepest abyss, they can reclaim life and spin darkness into light. That is certainly true in the case of Rena Quint.

The Jerusalemite has no knowledge of her genetic background. Try as she might, she cannot remember her biological parents or her two brothers who were killed in the Holocaust. "Nothing. I've tried so hard," she says mournfully.

Yet Rena was taken care of, time and again. She attracted many surrogate mothers and blossomed into a gem herself – a loving, giving, cheerful soul who at this time has four children, 22 grandchildren and five great-grandchildren. Photos of all of them line the walls of her home. In one, her husband, Emanuel, an American-born rabbi and lawyer, mugs with Hillary Clinton. In another, he and some of the grandchildren are parasailing in Eilat.

When as a child, Rena entered Bergen-Belsen, a

concentration camp in Germany, a soldier pried family photos out of her hand and tore them up. Her father had given them to her. With them, any visual reminders of her family of origin vanished forever.

Perhaps, she says, that is why so many family photos cover the surfaces of her house today.

The night before granddaughter Chamutal's wedding, Rena recounts her story, bridging the vast chasm between the horrors of the Holocaust and the joys of Jerusalem.

The conversation begins with a question about when her birthday is – and a most unusual answer.

"I have two birthdays. I have to explain that to you. I was adopted six times. I lost my mother and my brothers, Yossi and David, at around age 4. After the war, I went to Sweden in 1945. A woman who lost her daughter in the war asked me to be her daughter, and was going to the U.S. She brought me to the U.S. I got her daughter's name, birthday, where she was born, and we came to the U.S.

"I had this birthday from 1945 to 1989: February 15, 1936 ... In 1989, I went to Poland with Yad Vashem and found my real birth certificate: December 18, 1935. Now my kids make me two sets of parties, two sets of gifts and all that."

Thanks to help from the International Committee of the Red Cross, Rena learned that her name originally was Fredzia Lichtenstein and that she was born in Piotrkow, Poland, to Icek and Sala. Her parents, two brothers and she lived in what became the first Jewish ghetto.

"When the ghetto started, my father was taken to work at a glass factory. People were dying of starvation and sickness, but not fast enough, so they started an action. The soldiers broke down the doors and made everybody go out. You were chased out of your house; people were falling over each other.

"We were rounded up in the large courtyard that we had. We were herded through the streets like animals, being beaten, some falling down, until we were brought to the synagogue.

There everybody was crying and wailing. Nobody knew what to expect. People were being beaten and shot.

"On the other side of the sanctuary was a man, who I believe was my uncle, and he beckoned to me and he told me to run. I don't know how I was willing to leave my mother or how she was willing to leave me. I don't know how it happened – if she pushed me, if God pushed me. I ran out. That whole group of hundreds, maybe thousands of people, were sent to Treblinka. There they were gassed and their bodies burned.

"This man, my uncle, took me back to my father. He hid me for a while. When that was no longer feasible, he cut my hair and dressed me as a boy and named me Froim, and I worked with him in the glass factory. I got away with a lot of things. Otherwise, I wouldn't be here. We worked very hard. I always was lucky people helped me. I couldn't have done it without them.

"One day they decided they no longer wanted us in the factory. We were rounded up and taken to the station, where there were cattle cars waiting for us. We were in the cars many days, with no place to move around, no food, no water, and one waste pail that filled up very quickly. I remember the smell of it. People died. There were window openings with barbed wire on them. Icicles formed; people lifted others up to get air and get an icicle to drink.

"After what seemed like a lifetime, the trains stopped. They threw dead bodies into the snow. The rest of us had to jump out after them. We drank and ate the snow, washed our faces in the snow, and relieved ourselves in the snow. While we were getting used to this new scene, German soldiers with sidecars drove up with megaphones and said we were being transferred to camps, women on one side and men on another. My father realized if I got undressed, they would kill him; they would kill me for pretending to be a boy. He met a schoolteacher and asked her to keep an eye on me. He gave me some things, including some pictures, and he promised to meet me after the war in Piotrkow. He never kept that promise. I never saw him again. I don't think he ever got there. I never got there."

The schoolteacher became Rena's new mother. It was snowy and cold when they arrived at Bergen-Belsen. After Rena and her caretaker went through the showers, the woman stole a black coat that kept them warm and possibly saved their lives. The concentration camp was so crowded that they did not have enough room to sleep in the barracks, so they lay on the stone floor crawling with rats and lice.

Rena does not know what happened to the woman or to the black coat. She does remember how it felt as a child to live with fear, cold and hunger. The smell of vile soup and bread made of sawdust and moldy flour has stayed with her all these years.

"I still don't believe how I could have survived. I think it was a miracle and God meant for me to survive. The epidemics of typhus, pneumonia and dysentery were immense. One day I was very, very sick with typhus. There were no antibiotics, clothes or warm drinks. I was sitting under a tree. I couldn't get up. People were shouting, 'We're free.' The British liberated Bergen-Belsen in April 1945, and because there were so many sick people, they set up a makeshift hospital on the grounds of the concentration camp. I was put in there with the children."

Sweden opened its doors to 6,000 refugees of German concentration camps. Rena counts herself lucky, because she was able to go with a group of women and children to a displaced persons camp there. At age 9, she was very sick and taken to a hospital, where a Christian man wanted to adopt her. Adults who were watching out for her said she was Jewish and needed to go to Palestine with the orphans. But fate had a different plan in store.

A woman named Anna Philipstahl took her to America on the papers of her own dead daughter. Rena had met Anna and her son, Sigmond, in the displaced persons camp. Before the war, the woman had received documents from her brother for herself, her daughter and her son.

"Her daughter had died, and Anna now had an extra ticket

to America, and I had the good fortune to be picked by her to replace her daughter."

Unfortunately, Anna passed away three months after they arrived in the United States, and Rena was at a total loss. "I didn't understand at all," she laments. "They dug a grave; everybody around it cried. In Bergen-Belsen nobody cried. We went home and sat shiva (a ritual of seven days of intense mourning) for Anna. Her relatives who brought us over didn't want to keep me."

However, Anna's relatives knew a childless couple in Brooklyn who might be prepared to take in the girl for the Jewish Sabbath. Their names were Jacob and Leah Globe. Leah was 46 at the time. That weekend turned into a lifetime commitment, as the Globes adopted Rena and at last provided her with a permanent family.

She reflects, "I grew up as a normal American kid who never talked about the Holocaust. I didn't want to talk about it. Who would want to play with somebody who had had lice and fleas and dysentery?"

Rena does not remember the number the Germans assigned to her at Bergen-Belsen and engraved on her dog tag. She bears no tattoos and explains that only survivors of the Auschwitz concentration camp had prisoner numbers tattooed on their arms.

Her Holocaust experience was unlike that of others, she says. "My story is different – first, because a million children perished and I'm here. Second, most children survived because of false papers or in hiding with Christians. I did not.

"Mine was also different because every time I lost a mother, someone else came to take care of me. I got a new mother. I was lucky because I always had a woman to take care of me. It works that way; things just fall into my lap."

Rena enjoyed stability as a child and adult in America. She met Emanuel, her husband-to-be, in October 1958 on the holiday of Simchat Torah, the end of the harvest festival Sukkot, when people in the neighborhood were going from home to home for parties. They married in March 1959 and had a good life in Brooklyn before moving to Israel in 1982.

Ardent Zionists, they feel blessed with a rich life in the Holy Land. "We love living here. We're both involved in a lot of organizations. We feel it's important to help others. There's a lot of socializing, which we enjoy.

"We feel Israel is a Jewish state. If we had been living in America, we would have been celebrating Halloween this week, but here everybody comes out on Purim. We live very Jewish lives. Every Saturday is a holiday. We go to synagogue, Hovevei Zion.

"Being retired, we have a chance to go to many classes. My husband teaches Gemara (oral Torah) to retired men. My daughter teaches Psalms. I went to class with her this morning. Our kids all got married here in Israel. Our oldest daughter met her husband here. We have four grandkids in the Israeli Army at the moment."

Rena takes her philosophy about living life to its fullest to heart. She rejoices in the opportunity to be the Jew her fellow concentration camp inmates never had the chance to be.

"I feel Hitler wanted to kill all the Jews. He didn't succeed. But by assimilating and intermarrying, we're helping him. I would like to see everybody marry a Jewish spouse. It's easier here in Israel, if you're interested. And we are."

Clara Hammer

Born Winograd, Former Soviet Union
1910 – 2010

Clara Hammer

The Chicken Lady Of Jerusalem

I hadn't seen the "Chicken Lady" in eight years. We first met after the summer I spent at ulpan, an intensive Hebrew language program at Hebrew University in Jerusalem. I was looking for story ideas to pitch to Sam Orbaum, who was then the features editor at the Jerusalem Post, where I wanted to break in as a freelancer. During High Holiday services, the rabbi of a synagogue on Agron Street mentioned the "Chicken Lady" in his sermon about people doing good deeds. Later, I tracked down spunky Chaya Clara Hammer, who became my first story for the Post.

Now it was winter in Jerusalem, and Clara had a bad cold. But she insisted on the telephone, "I'll put on my makeup and my smile and I'll be fine. Come on over." The next day at her dining room table, the nerve center of her tzedaka, or charity, operation, the bubbly "Chicken Lady of Jerusalem" offered orange juice, sweets and her usual good cheer.

At 94, the "Chicken Lady of Jerusalem" has a lot to smile about. The great-great-grandmother enjoys a large extended family and an even larger brood of friends, many of whom she doesn't know. Clara Hammer feeds hundreds of poor families in Israel every week through her charity fund.

While she remains anonymous to most of them, Clara visits the Russian immigrants under her wing. Born in Russia in 1910, she enjoys keeping in touch with others from the motherland and seeing if they need anything she can provide – from a hearing aid to school supplies.

Once when a Russian immigrant lost an eye to cancer, Clara helped pay for a glass replacement. Somehow, every week the money comes through for these acts of kindness.

It all started in 1980 as she stood in line at Alti Hacker's butcher shop in Jerusalem to buy her Shabbat, or Sabbath, order. Clara delights in reliving the scene:

"There were two women ahead of me and two women in back of me. And in front was a young girl; I judged her to be about 13. And he handed her this huge bag of plastic that you put on the counter. I could see that all there was in there was fat, skins of chickens, some bones. And she said, 'Todah – Thank you,' and walked out.

"I was curious to know what she does with that junk, I would call it. Because when I buy a chicken, I tell him to please take off the whole skin because it has cholesterol. And so do other people."

When it was her turn, Clara asked the butcher, "How many cats or dogs does that family have?" He explained the family had many children and the father was on dialysis. Because of their financial difficulties, they had run up a tremendous bill. So the butcher now just gave them fat and skins for a soup for Friday night and a cholent, or stew, for Saturday.

Meanwhile, the women behind her began yelling, "Geveret, geveret," or "Lady, lady, let's go." Clara said, "Rega," or "Wait."

"I felt that I had something of great importance to accomplish," she recalls in English. "I said to Mr. Hacker, 'From today on, throw that stuff into the garbage. And give the family two chickens, a kilo of meat – it can be chopped or regular – and some very, very good turkey bones. Because I also use them in cholent or soup. And I will pay you.'"

And the Clara Hammer Chicken Fund took wing. Soon, the butcher began telling her about other families who needed help. Rabbis, social workers and friends sent referrals. Sometimes Clara initiated her own searches. For instance, when she heard about a family whose mother had committed suicide, she dispatched a granddaughter to that neighborhood.

The granddaughter found a neighbor to serve as a liaison with the family. The neighbor would take the family chicken for Shabbat until the man felt strong enough again to remarry.

Clara always has tried to follow the medieval Jewish philosopher Maimonides' principles of charity, the highest form of which is to help someone get back on his feet so that he no longer needs to depend on others.

On a limited budget herself, the pensioner receives Social Security income from her 40-year career as a Hebrew teacher in the United States. She couldn't keep providing chickens out of her own pocket, so she spread word to her three children and 10 grandchildren, and little by little the fund grew.

How many donors? "Who can count? Hundreds, for sure. Most of them are from America. And in America, it's mostly from Florida." She gestures toward her old-fashioned filing system – a stack of boxes that look like recipe containers. They hold index cards with names and addresses of donors across the globe.

The "Chicken Lady" treasures poems and letters from her public. A newly engaged couple once sent $200 with a note asking her to share their joy with those less fortunate. Clara obliged by taking a group of Russians out to a restaurant and topping off the meal with vodka.

She easily empathizes with people who are hungry, sick

or needy. "So when I hear of close to a million hungry families – you hear it, you read it in the papers – and I can help some of the children, I remember. I remember being chased out of Russia at the age of 10, getting to the borderline of Russia and Romania: a river."

Clara and her family had survived three pogroms in the Ukraine before running away. They could cross into Romania only when the river was frozen. So she, her father, mother, sister and brother waited. Finally, in a blanket of deep snow, the water froze, and they crossed.

"My mother was short of breath, and she fell in the snow. They wouldn't let my father go pick her up. And they arrested us and put us into prison in Romania.

"Five months, we were in prison. Just imagine not knowing where my mother is. And my mother, this poor woman, not knowing where her husband and her three children are."

Jews in Romania heard about the family and paid a lot of money to redeem them. The family told the Romanian Jews the story, and they put out a search and found Clara's mother in a hospital. The reunited family came to Palestine and lived in a tent for three years. But because the mother had contracted tuberculosis, they were advised to live in America for better hospital care.

Clara's empathy extends from the hungry to orphans. "I remember being handed food when we were hungry in Romania. And I know what it means to be motherless at the age of 15."

In her 94th year, Clara and her chicken fund were nurturing 252 families, many of whom went directly to the butcher to receive chicken, meat or liver, or a substitute if they happened to be vegetarian.

The "Chicken Lady" also was sending money to more than 100 needy families every month. "I send out every erev Rosh Hodesh (beginning of the new month) a check wrapped in a paper that says, 'Hodesh Tov – Have a good month.' So how can you wish a Hodesh Tov with an empty envelope? So you put in a check, according to the size of the family or the needs of the family. If it's a family with 11 children, or it's a family whose father was on a bus and killed by a suicide bomber … it can be from 250 shekels every single month up to 600." That translated to about $60 to $150 in American dollars.

An observant Jew who covers her hair with a wig and dresses modestly, Clara frequently cites Torah to make a point. Torah says to help one who puts out a hand for help. "Any family that turns to me for help, capital H-E-L-P, I trust them, and I help them.

"The need is tremendous. You read in newspapers. You hear on radio. You see on television. But some people just give an 'oy,' and they shut off the radio, shut off the television, put away the newspaper."

Again, she quotes Torah: "It says that a good name is better than good oil. And Baruch Hashem – Praise God, I have a good name. They know that every shekel I get goes to the charity fund."

Sara Lanesman

Sign Language Teacher
Born 1957, Colombecher, Algeria

Sara Lanesman

A Voice In Silence

One of the first people I knew who had moved from America to Israel was Norma Joffe. She grew up on the next block in our assimilated neighborhood in Tennessee, heard the Zionist call in the 1960s, went to work on a kibbutz (collective community) in Israel and came back only to visit family and friends. She also resided in the States for five years when her husband, Gadi Horev, did part of his medical studies and preparation there.

They live in Kfar Saba, where Norma works in a vocational high school for deaf Jewish and Arab pupils. It is the only school in Israel that teaches sign language.

Norma introduced me to her colleague, a sign language teacher named Sara Lanesman, and kindly served as interpreter. Through a mixture of English, Hebrew, sign language and laughter, we bridged cultures to present Sara's story.

ara Lanesman seems to dance through life with an open mind and heart. She exudes a passion for learning, and knows four kinds of sign language: Hebrew, Arabic, and British and American English.

A colleague at Beit Sefer Meyuchad Onim, the Amal Vocational High School, calls Sara one of the most in-demand sign language teachers in Israel.

Sara, who also teaches about the deaf culture in which she grew up, has written a book on sign language. Fellow teachers at the school for hearing-impaired Jewish and Arab children use it in class, along with a disk and workbook she developed to combine Hebrew and sign language.

She emphasizes that sign language is not universal. Not long ago in Israel, for instance, residents of different cities communicated with different sign languages. Her oldest sister lives in Haifa and speaks a different version than Sara does in the Tel-Aviv area.

The two come from a family of 12 siblings – four of whom cannot hear. Born in Algeria, Sara remembers many deaf villagers in her area. Ironically, in the deaf community in Israel, she encountered the most discrimination.

As she explains, "Most of the deaf population were educated people from Europe. They were afraid of us Algerians. We had a secret sign language that they considered crude."

Sara moved to Israel at age 5 1/2 with her family. She says during the war between France and Algeria, it was a dangerous time for Jews in her mostly Muslim native land.

Ironically, as a young girl, Sara didn't realize she was Jewish. "My first memory of religion was when we fled Algeria and sailed for France. I can still recall the large gathering of men on the boat, all of them bending forward in a rocking motion and praying."

Sara then began hearing stories from her parents and siblings about discrimination toward Jews in Algeria.

Soon in Israel, she ran across prejudice, but it was toward

her as a deaf person rather than as a Jew. "Since I was a child," she muses, "I have always tried to be an educator. When kids in my neighborhood would ask me to talk to laugh at me or make strange signs to mock my sign language, I would try to teach them sign language, try to explain to them that deaf people are normal."

Sara found a new means of expression at 14. That's when she joined a dance troupe called Kol V' De'mama, or Voice in Silence.

"We deaf feel music vibrations, especially on a wood floor. But that is not enough for dancing. We spent a lot of time learning rhythms, counting. Someone would beat out time on the floor with a long wooden stick. We learned to feel the rhythms and have an inner count."

Continuing to embrace the pleasure of movement, Sara choreographs dances that incorporate sign language. One year for Holocaust Remembrance Day in the city of Holon, she and a friend honored deaf victims of Nazi persecution by building a dance to the song "Every Man Has a Name."

Sara also helped prepare an exhibit for the deaf at the children's museum in Holon. "An Invitation to Silence," led by deaf guides, highlighted non-oral communication skills that exist in everyone, and which are best expressed in the absence of voice and sound. Visitors could discover an alternative world of expression, through hand movement and body language.

The mother of two also gives birth to her creativity through storytelling performances at an annual festival in Givatayim.

Although her son, Nadav, and daughter, Ya'ara, are able to hear, Sara talked to them in sign language from the moment of their births. "They were already signing themselves by 7 months," she says proudly. "They know from research that it helps kids as babies. So many people have said, 'If my kid speaks sign language, he's not going to talk.' But now they say, 'It's a shame we didn't also teach our kids sign language.'"

The skill comes in handy. For instance, Nadav had the

opportunity to travel to China as an interpreter for championship deaf players at an important basketball game.

Sara admits she wasn't active in the deaf community as a young woman. "One day, in 1981, a girlfriend dragged me to the Deaf Club in Tel-Aviv. There I met David, my husband."

As if her family, work and creative endeavors weren't enough, Sara keeps her mind sharp with learning. She holds an education degree and a certificate in group work with the deaf. Research intrigues her, particularly in the field of linguistics.

She has immersed herself in research on deaf Algerian Jews. Explaining the intrigue, she says, "It was a secret language. Until this day, there's no book, nothing. They know everything from oral tradition."

The fear that the Algerian sign language would disappear compelled her to work on a book with a Haifa University professor.

Sara's dance between tradition and modernity also pops up on the deaf scene in Israel. She is part of a group that has been helping make one sign language standard for the whole country.

"The new language has conquered the old language people brought from all the different countries they came from. That is, Hebrew sign language has taken over."

Lior Sasson

Heart Surgeon
Born 1960, Neve Monoson, Israel

Lior Sasson

Saving A Child's Heart

It's 6 a.m. the first Monday in November, and my favorite taxi driver is whisking me to the Edith Wolfson Medical Center in Holon, Israel, to witness open-heart surgery on a little girl from Angola. I am scheduled to meet Dr. Lior Sasson, director of the Cardiothoracic Department and head of the Pediatric Cardiac Surgery Unit, at 7 a.m. as he prepares for the operation. My taxi pulls up to the pediatric emergency room just as the heavens open and rain begins drenching the parched land. Lior is waiting at the entrance and politely ushers me into the windowless bowels of the hospital, where we will remain all morning, oblivious to the weather.

He is the lead surgeon for Save a Child's Heart, an Israeli-based international humanitarian program offering top-rate cardiac care for children from developing countries. Lior and his team believe every child – regardless of nationality, religion, sex or family financial situation – deserves the best medical treatment possible. This is one of the many good stories about Israel that garner too little attention.

I literally will be looking over Lior's shoulder

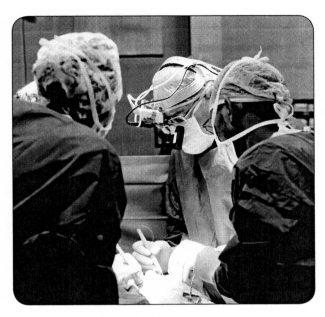

during the entire operation, as he and a colleague open Rosalinda's sternum and repair the holes in her heart that have made her young life a struggle.

I owe this privilege to my colleague, David Silverman, an Israeli photojournalist with whom I have been collaborating on this book. He had an established relationship with Save a Child's Heart from reporting on the program, enabling me to easily meet Lior, put on scrubs and observe the procedure being performed on tiny Rosalinda.

At 4 years old, she weighed only 11 kilos, or 24 pounds. Diagnosed with "failure to thrive," she had what the doctors call a Swiss cheese ventricular septal defect, or VSD, which means she had holes in the chest wall that separates the lower chambers of the heart. She had always rallied most of her energy for breathing rather than eating. Thanks to Lior and his team, she should have a normal life expectancy.

D r. Lior Sasson exudes calm even while holding a life in his hands. The lead surgeon for Save a Child's Heart operates on children from Angola to Zanzibar who otherwise would not have the medical care they need.

The Israeli doctor painstakingly makes minute incisions and stitches in a child's heart, while describing the steps in English for an observer and directing his medical team.

"I'm never calm," he admits hours after the open-heart surgery. "Maybe it looks like this. But every operation has its own stress, its own tension. I think it's healthy stress because it keeps you sharp. There are so many unknown variables in surgery, so I'm always worried about something. The thing is to trust yourself and your team and to make cardiac surgery routine, make it boring, so everyone knows what the next step is, the sequence of events."

Just after 8 a.m., an anesthesiologist puts 4-year-old Rosalinda to sleep so she will feel nothing and have no memory of the operation. Her figure limp on the operating table, she is hooked up to a cardiopulmonary bypass machine, which will take over the function of the heart and lungs during surgery.

Then Lior and another heart surgeon open Rosalinda's chest, splitting the sternum in half with an oscillating saw. We can see her heart beating through a hole in her brown skin. The doctors use solution to arrest her heart – flat-line it – so it will not beat while they are working inside of it.

Quietly, methodically, the doctors use scissors to open her heart – and are surprised to find more holes than expected. They patch and seal each one with a surgical cloth called a GORE-TEX graft. It's just after 10:30 a.m., and appropriately, somewhere in the room Louis Armstrong is belting out "What a Wonderful World" over the music system. "I see trees of green, red roses too. I see them bloom, for me and you. And I think to myself, what a wonderful world. I see skies of blue, and clouds of white. The bright blessed day, the dark sacred night. And I think to myself, what a wonderful world. ..."

It's a dark morning. Outside, sheets of rain pound the Tel-Aviv area; but inside, the pediatric operating room remains a calm sea of green. Little Rosalinda lies still on sterile green sheets as the doctors and assistants tie off her stitches. They wean her from the cardiopulmonary bypass machine, allowing her heart to circulate blood and her lungs to breathe again. After making sure her organs function properly, they close her chest.

Lior leaves the operating room at 11:46 a.m., keeping on his glasses but removing the loops over them that magnify everything fourfold when he is performing surgery. He heads down the hall for a quick lunch of hummus and pita.

We talk in the staff lounge about Rosalinda's prognosis. "Now she will be like any other kid. She will have a normal life expectancy," he says. "This is a real lifesaving operation. Otherwise, she would die at age 20."

He humbly credits his team for helping to make such a difference in a child's life possible, from the cardiologists who diagnose problems to the perfusionists who set up and operate the heart-lung machine that keeps patients alive while their heart is stilled for an operation.

Poor children like Rosalinda who were born with congenital heart defects come to Israel from all over the world to receive medical care not available to them otherwise. Donors to Save a Child's Heart cover the expenses. Dr. Ami Cohen founded the Israel-based humanitarian program in 1995 on the belief that every child, regardless of nationality, religion, gender or financial ability, deserves the best medical treatment available.

Lior became lead surgeon of Save a Child's Heart when Cohen, his mentor, died suddenly in 2001, a day after conquering the summit of Mount Kilimanjaro. "He changed my life, actually," reflects Lior. "I was his first assistant. After I was introduced to this fascinating subspecialty of pediatric cardiac surgery, he sent me to Ann Arbor, Michigan, for another two years of training, and he was waiting for me to come back."

In 2000, after completing the fellowship in pediatric cardiac surgery, Lior returned to his native Israel and to Wolfson Medical Center, where he had done his residency after studying medicine at Ben-Gurion University of the Negev. In addition to assisting Cohen in the pediatric cardiac unit at Wolfson, he became a lead surgeon in the adult cardiac unit. In 2007, Lior was named chief of the Cardiothoracic Department.

Wearing his hat as lead surgeon for Save a Child's Heart, Lior travels around the world evaluating sick children, performing surgeries and following up on former patients. A few days after operating on Rosalinda, he packed his bags for China.

"We try to follow the aim of Ami Cohen's heart," Lior explains. "He was posted in Korea, and was asked by the locals to assist the natives with heart programs. He performed a few closed-heart surgeries over there. He had a passion for helping kids without economic abilities. His first aim was establishing competent centers and bringing local teams to Israel to practice their training."

Both the patients and the medical teams make up the international mosaic that is Save a Child's Heart. Beginning his rounds at 7 a.m. before Rosalinda's procedure, Lior passes in the hall a 14-year-old boy from Gaza who has recently undergone emergency surgery for a tumor on his trachea. The doctor then checks patients in the intensive care unit, including a 2-month-old boy from Gaza with a heart lesion. The team from Save a Child's Heart put in a shunt to help the baby breathe.

Gaza lacks the trained personnel, equipment and medical facilities required for such cardiac surgery, according to Lior. His teams have operated on 2,200 children, half of them Palestinians. "I see it as seeds for peace, because I think every family who was treated here and went home, they know what we did for them. Their tribe knows and their village knows. I think someday it will bring peace closer."

He might say the same about Iraqis. Lior's colleagues from Save a Child's Heart go to Jordan specifically to screen Iraqis, seeing as many as 40 to 50 patients in one day. "We have already operated on 60 kids, maybe more, from Iraq. It's like closing a circle," he adds when I point out the irony that his parents emigrated from Iraq in 1949.

Lior, whose name means "my light" in Hebrew, was born in Israel in 1964. His mother said her baby was a light for her. She could see his future as a doctor early on.

His career path has brought some unusual twists. During the Lebanon War in 2006, the father of an Iraqi child Lior had operated on called to make sure the doctor was safe from rocket fire.

The gesture made an impression. As Lior, a former Israeli Navy captain, says, "A great relationship evolved." Other parents have named children after him. Sometimes the mothers of children whose lives he helped save will keep in touch by sending photos throughout the years.

On screening missions to different countries, Lior sees for himself the former patients who have grown up, married, had children and even followed in his footsteps. One woman in Ethiopia who had surgery in Israel as a teenager chose to become a doctor.

A father of three, Lior counts his blessings. "I am in a special position of being able to make a difference. Sometimes, I work in the ICU and see kids and realize if we didn't operate on them, they would have died. There is nothing compared to seeing the smile of a child who's healthy, to see his mother, to see the life he's giving to another – it's beyond any words."

Liora Tedgi

Founder Of Ohr Meir & Bracha:
The Terror Victims Support Center
Born 1965, Jerusalem, Israel

Liora Tedgi

Turning Tests Into Strength

Yehoyariv is a tiny street in the religious neighborhood of Arzei Habira in Jerusalem. Here I have been studying Torah with Rebbetzin Chana Poupko almost every week since the winter of 2005. Well, she has been here. I have been in Tennessee. The miracles of modern technology have allowed us to learn together by telephone. For a while, she had an American line, meaning I paid only long-distance rates instead of overseas rates for our calls. If I was on the road at our appointed time, I could simply pull over to a gas station, dial Chana on my cell phone, and learn for 10 or 20 minutes, closing the gap between the Southern United States and Israel – not to mention the second millennium and Biblical times.

Chana and her family hosted me during a summer visit in Israel when the lilac trees were in bloom and fresh apricots in abundance. Rounding the corner to their apartment building one day, I noticed the Terror Victims Support Center on the corner of Yehoyariv and Yakim Street. That's when I met Liora.

Liora Tedgi is a tiny woman whose oversize black hat and purposeful energy spell seriousness. Fueled by personal tragedy, this terror victim has transformed her pain into a touchstone for service.

In 2002, she was handing out food to the needy in Jerusalem's Beit Israel neighborhood when a suicide bomber detonated a car in front of her. Nearby, a group of women with baby carriages had been waiting for their husbands to finish the evening prayers.

Moshe Suissa, commander of Jerusalem's Fire and Rescue Service, had witnessed many terrorist attacks in Jerusalem. But never had he seen one so horrendous.

"I was the first on the scene," he recalled in an Israel United Appeal article. "There were 10 dead. Three of the bodies were literally on fire, including a baby, about a year old. The first thing I did was to pick up the baby and hold her up to my body in order to put out the fire. Then I ran with her to the Magen David Adom ambulance for emergency medical treatment. Her mother was running after me the whole time, trying to see her baby. But I couldn't let her; it was too shocking."

Liora, who was pregnant, also went into shock and couldn't move. She recalls people screaming. "Every mother started looking at her stroller to see if the baby was there."

Her husband, father and two brothers were also at the scene. "It's very hard to explain what you feel after the bombing. I was angry. I didn't understand. My husband was in bed one year."

Devastated, Liora realized she needed to channel her energy in positive ways. She asked God for help and prayed at the graves of righteous persons for direction.

A year and a half after the bombing, Liora became pregnant – again – with twins. Meanwhile, because of their own family history, she and her husband, Nissim, decided to establish an organization to help terror victims. They called it Ohr Meir & Bracha (a light that illuminates and blessing).

A mother of 10, Liora says, "You have to turn suffering into strength." She is on intimate terms with both. Terrorist attacks have killed or injured eight members of her family.

Liora puts her moxie to use assisting other terror victims who have fallen through the cracks of Israeli bureaucracy. As she says, "I think it's my shlichut (mission) to help people."

Ohr Meir & Bracha: The Terror Victims Support Center helps families and individuals in crisis, offering food, clothes, school supplies, an after-school program, household appliances, psychological and legal services, and financial assistance. Most clients live near or below the poverty level. The financial burden, coupled with physical and emotional trauma in the aftermath of terrorist attacks, has pushed many to the brink of collapse.

The center runs on donations from Israel and abroad. Volunteer labor helps keep costs low – particularly on Thursday afternoons, when food basket assembly lines fill little Yakim Street. People spill into the neighborhood to pack challas (loaves of bread for the Sabbath or holidays), zucchini, eggplant, tomatoes, apples, oranges, canned sardines, sweet corn, sugar, jam, crackers, tea, coffee, chicken soup mix and other staples.

To support northern Israel, where Katyusha rockets fell during the Lebanese war in summer 2006, Ohr Meir & Bracha took two truckloads of food to thousands of families, along with supplies like soap, shampoo, sheets, pillows, towels, formula and diapers. The center also provided housing in central and southern Israel for hundreds of families fleeing the north.

Beyond the basics of shelter and food, Liora and her caring troops offered hope. They arranged activities and outings to improve quality of life for the northern Israelis – from a bar mitzva ceremony at the Western Wall to a children's trip to the Jerusalem Biblical Zoo.

Day to day, the organization born out of Liora's own pain helps Israelis one to one. They're people like Alon, a terror victim with many debts who is on the verge of a nervous breakdown; Yechezkel, who is looking after several small children because his wife is very ill; and David, who has no food at home. They're children in the Jerusalem area who otherwise wouldn't be eating a hot daily meal.

Liora relates especially to the children. She grew up with three brothers in a poor family in Jerusalem. "Every week, I went to some organization to ask for food," she confides.

"When I needed to ask for food, I cried. I asked my mother, 'Why me?' She said, 'This is your responsibility. If you didn't bring the food, we would have nothing to eat.' She worked day and night, cooking, cleaning, washing other people's clothes by hand, caring for children.

"My father didn't see well. My mother didn't want to go to the government. She didn't want to take from someone else who might need help more, who couldn't work or was sick. She said, 'I work. It's hard, but I can work.'

"We never complained. My mother always taught us to be thankful for what Hashem (God) brings you. For everything. My mom taught us to trust Hashem."

People still seek out Liora's mother, the wife of a rabbi, to be blessed for everything from a peaceful home to the right marriage partner. Rebbetzin Shulamit Sara lives in Jerusalem with her daughter and family.

Liora also bestows blessings on those who request them. This is a tradition in her family.

One might see her work as a form of blessing. It's a Sunday, and Liora is busy with phone calls and visitors. She has found someone in England who wants to financially assist one bombing victim every month.

Liora dashes between the two small rooms in her office, signing checks, greeting supporters, telling stories about the terror victims her center helps.

Unfortunately, many couples want to divorce after surviving a bombing – especially if they lose a child. Liora blesses them for a peaceful home, and counsels both spouses. She found a husband a job as a truck driver because he was out of work. She found a housekeeper for a woman who had to stay in bed for nine months to heal from injuries suffered in an attack.

She even helped finance in-vitro fertilization for a woman whose child had died in a bus bombing. The bereaved mother didn't know whether she could become pregnant again. But she did. "Now she has comfort," Liora happily reports.

Then, sadly, she shows a picture of a girl wearing a brace to correct a spinal problem. "Time is of the essence. Every check I give them, they send a thank-you letter," says Liora, adding empathetically, "Without the brace, she'd be miserable all her life and couldn't even have children."

Sometimes Liora becomes frustrated with bureaucratic bumbling. As she explains, "After the bombings, people aren't normal, and they can't be normal. I had someone with 100 nails in his body. The government wanted him to work. We have a responsibility to care for our brothers."

Liora has taught this lesson to her children. She knows it has sunk in. As an example, her 12-year-old son paid for a schoolmate to go on a field trip he couldn't afford. The modest son didn't tell Liora this; his teacher did.

Her own mother's teachings about faith and gratitude for God's blessings guide Liora's work. As Liora says, "God promised Abraham, 'I will give this land to your descendants.' I bless all Am Yisrael (the nation of Israel), wherever they are, that Hashem is with us and helps us. B'ezrat Hashem (God willing), He will bring the messiah soon."

Sarah Nachshon

Activist – Volunteer
Born 1944, Kfar Hasidim, Israel

Sarah Nachshon

Taking A Stand In Hevron

Israel is a small country in more respects than geography. The American notion of "six degrees of separation" – that we are all connected by six stages of circumstance or acquaintance – shrinks to fewer degrees in Israel. My friend Noga is the niece of a world-famous Hasidic artist, Baruch Nachshon, with whom she arranges an interview for me. I board a bulletproof bus from Jerusalem to the gritty town of Kiryat Arba near Hevron, a ride of about an hour.

Baruch, sporting a beret and long beard, opens the door to his apartment, exchanges greetings and quickly retreats to the bedroom to lie down while enduring the pain of a kidney stone. His wife, Sarah, takes over as hostess. She has played the role many times before in the spirit of Abraham and Sarah, father and mother of the Jewish people known for their hospitality, and buried nearby in a Hevron cave. The Nachshons – famous in Israel as modern pioneers – have put up as many as 30 guests at a time in their apartment, providing them with meals and sleeping accommodations.

Sarah sits on the couch, framed by her husband's

paintings depicting the struggle between good and evil, and recounts stories of her hardscrabble life. Her pleasant face and quiet manner belie a feistiness that the tales reveal.

S arah and Baruch Nachshon are Sabras, the word for native Israelis that refers to a cactus: prickly on the outside and soft on the inside. The Nachshons embody both characteristics. They were among the pioneers responsible for renewing a Jewish presence in ancient Hevron for the first time since Arabs massacred Jews there on Aug. 24, 1929.

Their story and modern Hevron's are interwoven like a braided challa (loaf of bread for the Sabbath). After the Six-Day War in 1967, they defied various governments of Israel to bring Jews back to the City of the Patriarchs and Matriarchs – final resting place of Abraham and Sarah, Isaac and Rebecca, Jacob and Leah.

Sarah, mother of 10 and grandmother of more than 60 at this writing, recalls corresponding with the Lubavitcher Rebbe in New York after the miraculous Israeli victory in 1967. She and Baruch told the Rebbe, spiritual leader of the Chabad-Lubavitch Hasidic movement, they wanted to live in the newly liberated city of Hevron. Such historic locations that were off-limits for so many years were now under Israeli control. The Rebbe gave them a special blessing to settle there.

In 1968, the Nachshons went to Hevron with a group of people who stayed at an Arab hotel and celebrated Passover. They spent a week at the hotel, then told the government they wanted to stay. As Sarah recalls, the response was, "You cannot stay here because it's an Arab city."

Baruch remembers, "One of the officers told her and the others, 'The government can't swallow you and can't throw you out. You are like a bone stuck in the throat.'"

Sarah and her fellow pioneers weren't to be dissuaded. The

only safe place was in the Hevron Military Compound on a hill overlooking the city, where each family was given one large, empty room. Begun with seven families, the group lived like a small kibbutz, or collective community. The government thought they would be there a short time, surrounded by the Arabs of Hevron, surrounded by barbed wire.

What the government couldn't understand was the pioneers' determination that presented as stubbornness. "We came back after the Six-Day War as God had given us all the holy places there," says Sarah. "So we came to our fathers and mothers in Hevron."

Doggedly remaining for 3 1/2 years, the group grew to 35 families and had no more room. "So the government built Kiryat Arba for us. It's a city down from Hevron. No houses were here. An empty place. We didn't take anybody from his house. It was an empty mountain."

Established in 1971, the suburb of Hevron lies five minutes from the Cave of Machpelach, burial site of Abraham and Sarah, Isaac and Rebecca, Jacob and Leah.

In 1968, Sarah had the first Jewish child born in Hevron since the massacre. They named him Shneur Hevron. "It means two lights in Hevron: one that was covered in the big massacre and now a new light that is coming to Hevron."

There was great excitement. The president of Israel and the mayor of Jerusalem sent telegrams. Menachem Begin was named Shneur's godfather. Knesset members showed up, and Prime Minister Levi Eshkol sent a representative to help celebrate the circumcision. Sarah had in mind a special ceremony.

"I wanted to make the bris (circumcision ceremony) in the Cave of Machpelach, near the tomb of our Father Abraham. But I had a special delivery from the defense minister that I could not make the bris in the Cave of Machpelach because of wine."

She explains that Muslims, also descendants of Abraham, held the tomb as their shrine as well, and didn't allow wine. So the Nachshons had their son's circumcision ceremony in the police station. For others, it would have been an unlikely locale, but the station had served as Sarah's dwelling place in her quest to repopulate Hevron with Jews.

With the birth of her next son, Sarah realized her dream. She held his bris in the Cave of Machpelach without permission, with wine. "The day after, it was in all the papers that in this town in Israel, there was a secret mission – the first bris in the Cave of Machpelach – and it was very successful," she says triumphantly.

Her ninth child's bris in Machpelach was not such a victory. In the middle of the ceremony, an army officer appeared, seized the bottle of wine and took away Baruch Nachshon for fingerprinting. In the ensuing confusion, the wine disappeared, and without the evidence, the army had to release Sarah's husband.

The pioneering couple named their baby Avraham. "This child passed away in a crib death at 6 months. I decided that this child was born here, we made the bris here, and he had to be buried here also in the old Jewish cemetery, where the Arabs broke all the stones and planted a vineyard," Sarah recounts.

"But the government didn't give permission to bury my son in the old Jewish cemetery. So I stayed in the road and refused to move for more than two hours until it was late at night. And I said to a big officer that came, 'You don't let me go? Okay, watch my car. I'm now taking my son in my hands, and I am going to the cemetery. Yes, you can watch my car.' And I started to walk.

"They ran to the walkie-talkie – they had no pelephones (mobile phones) at that time. And they said, 'Okay, you have a special order from the defense minister that he will let you bury your son in the old Jewish cemetery.'"

Friends from Kiryat Arba were waiting for her at the cemetery. Sarah hadn't prepared anything to say, but two ideas came to mind. First, she retold a story from the Gemara, or oral Torah: A child and his father went for a walk. The child was tired and the father put him on his shoulders. He asked, "Father, when are we coming to the city?" The father said, "My son, if you see a cemetery, you'll know we are close to the city."

Sarah drew a Hevron parallel, "It opened today, the old Jewish cemetery. I know that we are close now to having the city open once more for the Jewish people to return to reclaim their land."

Second, she pointed out that Abraham had bought the cave, Machpelach, for his wife, Sarah. "And my name is Sarah, and I brought my son Avraham to the cave 4,000 years later. This was happening – burying my son in Hevron was happening – to live inside Hevron."

Her words came true two years later, in 1979, when a group of 15 women and 35 children went to live inside Hevron. In the middle of the night, they took a truck and went to the back side of the old Beit Hadassah, the first hospital in Israel which the Jewish people had built more than 100 years previously.

The women cut barbed wire, put up a ladder and moved through a window frame with all the children, some of them in baby carriages. Sarah brought a supply of candies and cookies for the little ones. Husbands helped the women move in mattresses, portable stoves, chemical toilets, sacks of potatoes and other supplies.

When soldiers discovered the new residents early in the morning, they did not know what to do. Menachem Begin said he would not evacuate women and children by force. For two months, no one was allowed in, and anyone who left could not return. The Begin government, concerned about political and security issues, decided to allow the Jews to live in the heart of Hevron. Soon the women and children were permitted in and out, but no one could join them.

As Sarah reports, they had no water or electricity – only the will to rebuild Hevron. For months, people from Kiryat Arba brought them food through the windows.

Early on, her boy, Shneur, was ill with tuberculosis and a throat problem. Her husband says he wrote Begin that because of the cold and the rats, the boy was sick. He pleaded for mattresses and windows to keep out the cold. The day after receiving the letter, Begin gave permission to provide the group with mattresses and fix the windows.

Husbands could speak to the women through the windows. After three months, the government let the men come make the kiddush prayer (over wine or grape juice) on the Sabbath and stay for half an hour. After six months, husbands were permitted to join the women and children at Beit Hadassah. After a year, Sarah gave birth to a girl named Hadasse.

After a year, the government also gave permission for Jews to begin to rebuild a community in Hevron. Ensconced years later in her cozy Kiryat Arba apartment, Sarah reflects, "Now, because of this, because of all the women and children, Jewish people are living in Hevron."

She does not know all the residents of Kiryat Arba anymore. Now the Nachshons live among some 10,000 residents of the southern Hevron Hills communities. Kiryat Arba has drawn thousands of native Israelis as well as immigrants from America, India, Ethiopia and Russia.

There Sarah gives her husband the time to be an artist. Meanwhile, she stays busy with family and other activities. She volunteers to help senior citizens and makes a weekly trip to different Biblical sites.

"I have every day what to do. To make the house and to clean the house and to cook and to bake. We have, baruch Hashem (praise God), a new grandchild, and we have the bar mitzva of another grandchild. So I am busy all the time. I have no time to rest."

Says her husband: "I admire her and look at her spiritual image. It's a present from Heaven to me, and to the family and to the community."

Hanoch Teller

Author – Storyteller – Teacher
Born 1956, Vienna, Austria

Hanoch Teller

Telling Tales In And Out Of School

I first encountered Rabbi Hanoch Teller through his children. Half of them – nine of 18 siblings – came to dinner one Sabbath at my hosts' home in Jerusalem when Hanoch and his wife, Aidel, were out of town at a wedding. The Teller children were very sweet and well-mannered, which I thought spoke well of their parents. I know families with only one-sixth that number of children for whom I couldn't say the same.

The Tellers live in the apartment across the hall from my teacher, Chana, and her family, in a religious neighborhood of Jerusalem called Arzei Habira. I met Hanoch there the following year when I bought his new book, "Too Beautiful," and had him autograph it for a friend.

The next week, I had the pleasure of sitting with Hanoch in his study, where hundreds of Jewish books line the walls. I felt nervous about interviewing another author, especially a well-known one with interests close to my own. I like spotlighting colorful characters with inspiring stories to tell. And now I was sitting with a writer and storyteller who helped make popular the

Jewish literary genre of true, contemporary tales to convey inspirational and ethical themes.

Hanoch quickly put me at ease with his humor. I asked about a broken squash racket hanging on the wall behind his chair. An avid squash player, he laughed and sheepishly explained, "I missed the ball."

His professional life, though, has been a smash hit.

Principals, students, cab drivers and millionaires populate Hanoch Teller's stories, teaching us lessons in integrity, charity, faith and compassion.

Protagonists who illustrate the subject of divine providence include a man who misses a plane but saves his life and a yeshiva student who rescues a bum due to a long-forgotten school incident.

Teachers of faith in Hanoch's world range from an old rabbi in a rough New York neighborhood to a nonobservant Jewish soldier who prays spontaneously. The rabbi's shul (synagogue) survives attacks by hoodlums and evil attempts to appropriate the property. The soldier's tank crew is snatched from certain death in the Lebanese war.

Hanoch's first series of books, "Once Upon a Soul," "Soul Survivors," and "Souled!" introduced the genre of true, contemporary stories promoting themes of divine providence and human kindness. He branched out into biographies of contemporary Orthodox Jewish personalities, such as Rabbi Shlomo Zalman Auerbach and Baltimore, Maryland, Torah day school principal Rabbi Binyamin Steinberg, using anecdotes to teach morals and ethics.

From a small, cramped office in his home, Hanoch gives life to large characters such as Rabbi Steinberg, who knows every student in his school is a precious individual and an important young lady. He also knows that, unfortunately, not all the students realize this about themselves.

"Not every student could achieve a combined score of 1,400 on her SAT. But every student could excel at something," Hanoch writes. "Not every student was the daughter of a rosh yeshiva (head of a Jewish religious school), and not every student was destined to make her mark as a teacher, rebbetzin (rabbi's wife) and kollel (Torah study institute) wife. But every student could sanctify God's Name through careful observance of mitzvos (good deeds), chesed (kindness) and refined behavior. It was the school's responsibility to bring this message to its students – to each student individually. There was far more to schooling than just demanding excellence in studies."

Hanoch, a rabbi in his own right, began penning stories as a teenager. "Maybe subconsciously my name had something to do with it," quips the author of nearly 30 books.

Born in Vienna, Austria, in 1956, he grew up in Stamford, Connecticut. Just before World War II, Hanoch's father and his siblings had managed to escape to the United States; their parents had not. Hanoch's father returned to Austria after the Holocaust to see if he could salvage the family business, but then eventually the Tellers moved again to America.

By age 17, Hanoch already had finished college. "My sophomore, junior, senior years were all together," he says. Because he had a sharp memory and tested well, peers used to call him CLEP, the acronym for College Level Examination Program.

Hanoch graduated with a Bachelor of Arts degree in history after only a year and a half. He combined CLEP exams with studies at five universities at the same time – City College of New York, Columbia University, Hofstra University, New York University and Yeshiva University.

"I just wanted to get it over with," Hanoch says, referring to college, "because I wanted to come to Israel to learn." He had spent ninth grade in an Israeli high school.

His dream came true when he returned to Israel to learn in a yeshiva, an institution for study of traditional Jewish texts.

A group flight to Belgium cost $138. For an additional $100 to go from anywhere in Europe to Tel-Aviv, Hanoch thought he had found a sweet deal. The journey brought its share of drama, however, including an emergency landing in Newfoundland after a passenger, an American serviceman, suffered a heart attack. The serviceman's wife could not disembark with him in Newfoundland, because she would not have had money for a ticket to continue to Germany, where he was stationed.

Hanoch grabbed an airsickness bag and took up a collection to raise the required amount. As sometimes happens, he became part of the story he tells.

Once he landed in Israel, he wanted to do something else meaningful and traveled to Kiryat Shemona, a development town in the north, to teach Torah to unaffiliated Jews from America who were volunteering there.

However, the Jewish Agency rebuffed his attempts to reach out to the group through the agency's educational program. Hanoch found the situation appalling. "I felt I had to do something about it. I didn't know how to do anything but to write about it."

He submitted pieces to Moment Magazine and the Jewish Observer – thus sparking his writing career.

"People liked it and said, 'Why don't you write another one?' I was tapping talent I didn't know I had." He noticed that human-interest stories strongly captured his imagination.

Hanoch's year in Israel turned out to be a lifetime, because he never went back. In the course of his studies, he obtained rabbinic ordination from the former rabbi of the Western Wall, Meir Yehuda Getz.

Although never intending to be a pulpit rabbi, he did crave the discipline and learning that the challenging course of study provided.

The author sees a parallel in skills between writing and rabbinic studies. As he says, "My success as a prolific writer has been deadlines. I make a deadline and keep it. Semicha (ordination) is a goal. You're tested on a specific section of Shulchan Aruch (code of Jewish law)."

An avid learner, Hanoch decided to apply to journalism school at Columbia University because he had never formally studied writing, other than in English 101. To be admitted, he had to submit something he had published. He sent in three books he had written.

On the first day of class, the dean asked to see Hanoch. The dean had looked at Hanoch's books, said the man already knew how to write, and walked him to the bursar's office for a full refund.

"I say sometimes I was rejected by the Columbia School of Journalism," Hanoch says wryly.

The Orthodox Jewish lecturer and author has written hundreds of stories, essays and historical narratives, in addition to dozens of books. He also finds time to work as a teacher, producer, advisor and tour guide in Jerusalem.

How does he do it all? "One thing I don't do is sleep. I can't remember when I got more than three hours. I'm always tired."

Hanoch likes to say he and his wife gave up sleep – and privacy – when their family expanded. The couple, married since 1978, count one set of triplets and two sets of twins among their brood. The age range between the youngest and eldest of their 18 children is 21 years.

He sings Aidel's praises: "All the work with the kids, she does. I teach at women's seminaries, so when I'm gone, she's my substitute. She's the most remarkable person in the world; she's never raised her voice."

Hanoch also beams about the children. "They're always making me proud that they extend themselves for other people."

While he travels abroad 10 times a year doing storytelling and lecturing, Hanoch makes it a point to go to his children's schools before and after the trips.

"One rookie teacher said, 'This Teller kid must be an only child because his father always comes to check up on him.'"

When in town, Hanoch also carves out writing time in the mornings and learning time in the afternoons. For 30 years, he has been religious about studying at Mir Yeshiva near his home.

He wishes he could write more. Storytelling brings rewards as well – kind of like a runner's high, he says. "I am eager to make an impact on an audience. Often people wish to speak to me after a talk. Invariably, they want to tell me how they connect to my message."

His award-winning 1996 docudrama, "Do You Believe in Miracles," also has touched fans in many countries.

As if all that were not enough, Hanoch squeezes in time to perform the mitzva of matchmaking. Although not a professional, he has about 200 successful matches to his credit.

"I'm very concerned about the whole singles plight," he explains, adding that he recorded a CD on the topic. Because the rabbi teaches in several seminaries, he has a large pool from which to draw. "I'm in a good position to be of help. Factually, almost everybody is."

He pulls out a typewritten list from his wallet, showing single Jewish men's and women's names from Israel and America. Piled on his desk are interview notes from people who have sought his matchmaking assistance.

As he says, it would be irresponsible just to throw out names to them. "It takes fine-tuning and coaxing and cajoling and wheedling."

Wearing another of his many hats, Hanoch serves as one of the few independent guides licensed by Yad Vashem, Israel's Holocaust Martyrs' and Heroes' Remembrance Authority, to lead tours of its Holocaust Memorial Museum.

But that's another story.

Miri Flusser

Teacher
Born 1960, Jerusalem, Israel

Miri Flusser

Deep Roots In Israel And India

It's the week after Tu B'Shevat, the New Year of the Trees, and I am sitting at a dining room table in Jerusalem, munching delicious kumquats, dried figs, dates and almonds. This is usual fare that my Israeli hosts serve with tea when guests visit. I have just met Miri and Johanan Flusser, who are friends of a friend, and am grateful for their warmth and hospitality on this cold winter afternoon, because I am on my usual "no-car diet" in Israel. That means I walk a lot here, schlepping my laptop, snacks and sunscreen in a backpack and working up an appetite. The pounds melt off, but as soon as I return to my car and driving lifestyle in the United States, it is a struggle to log as many walking miles as I do here.

The Flussers represent what I love about Israel: a melting pot of cultures. Yesterday, I needed a tire repaired on a rental car, and struggled in broken Russian, Yiddish and Hebrew to make conversation with the elderly shop owner, who had moved to Israel from the Ukraine many decades ago. English carried me through the day's other meetings with Anglos from

America, Australia and Britain. We quickly learned about one another's culture by discussing TV shows, politics, family life and personal histories.

Wherever I turn, Israel is a sociology textbook. Spending a few hours with Miri Flusser is a chance to find out more about Sephardic culture – broadly, Jews descended from the Iberian Peninsula, and specifically in her case, the Jews of India.

T he Jews of Cochin, in South India, trace their roots back 2,000 years. Miri Flusser says she can trace hers back in Cochin at least six or seven generations.

Miri, a first-generation Israeli, has recently reclaimed her roots. Her grandparents decided to leave India to realize their dream of living in the new State of Israel in 1951.

Her mother, Sarah, came to Israel as a teenager when the family made aliya, or became citizens. They had left Cochin and waited in Bombay four years until Israel gave them permission to immigrate. Sarah had grown up religious in India and felt uncomfortable at her new school in Haifa, where the other girls didn't dress as modestly as she was accustomed to and wore short-sleeve or sleeveless tops.

At 16, Sarah went through an arranged marriage with a 30-year-old friend of her father. Both of their families were Zionists from India and lived in the same immigrant village on Israel's border with Jordan. Miri remembers hearing bombs exploding there as a child.

Miri's father, David, was well-educated and excelled in mathematics, but his lack of Hebrew skills limited his job opportunities. So he worked with sheep and chickens and farmed vegetables in the village.

Miri has inherited his green thumb, and proudly shows off the abundant garden that includes flowers, plants, and lemon and orange trees outside her suburban Jerusalem apartment. She also has chickens and a rabbit in the backyard.

Inside, flanked by dozens of marionettes that decorate her living room and hint at her playful spirit, Miri talks more about her roots. "My parents gave up the roles they would have had in Indian culture. It was very difficult to come to Israel. For my grandmother, it was a shock. In India, women don't go out to work. They work at home. It's like the way Ethiopian immigrants are struggling to adjust to living in this society today."

As a schoolgirl, Miri felt different, just as her mother had. "The teachers forced us to wear certain clothes. They said, 'Do it our way; wear what we do.' At that point, I decided to be a teacher. I wanted our religion to unite people instead of dividing them."

In the Israeli village where she grew up, Miri enjoyed living close to nature and felt that was a way to express her connection to God. Many other ways also have remained constants in her life, including Torah study and a focus on unity among different people.

After her service in the Israeli Army, Miri kept the promise she had made to herself and became a teacher. She earned a degree from the David Yellin Academic College of Education in Jerusalem, a multicultural institution and microcosm of Israel that brings together secular and religious Jews, Muslims and Christian Arabs.

"I'm not a regular teacher," asserts Miri, a 26-year veteran who sports cropped hair and a nezem, or nose jewel, that is an Indian custom, and dresses modestly in pants covered by a tunic. "I integrate subjects. I make it personal for the children. For example, if I teach about Jacob and Esau, I ask the children, 'Who's the oldest in your family? How do you feel about your position in the family?' In the Bible, you have everything – relationships between husbands and wives, siblings. It's not boring."

Miri teaches third- through seventh-graders at a religious school in the upscale Jerusalem neighborhood of Baka. She helps them learn respect for all creatures, both humans and animals – "because the Bible says God created man, not Jews or Arabs or Christians. ... There is nothing God created that isn't good. Everything has a purpose."

She teaches not only the required subjects, but also self-knowledge and love. As Miri explains, "I help children know themselves, their strong points, their weak points, and that we are not perfect. Oh, you're good at this; oh, you need to work on this. If you touch their heart, you can open their mind and they give you the sky."

Her current aim is to teach children emotional intelligence through a curriculum she developed. Miri speaks joyfully about her own inner work, having studied Imago relationship therapy and a technique for healing emotional stress that involves tapping on acupressure points.

A mother of four, Miri shows children ways to listen to one another so that everyone feels heard. "When I say I'm smart, it's egotistical; nobody can hear it. But when I say I'm smart in mathematics, they can hear it. Another says I am smart in English. They learn to be teachers and students to each other. Maybe the other does not like mathematics like you, but he is smart in different ways, maybe painting, swimming, something."

In 2009, Miri was one of 11 finalists for recognition as Israel's best teacher. Pupils, parents and other teachers selected them from among 3,000 contestants. The honor inspired Miri to begin writing a book about her teaching ideology and how she succeeds in touching children's hearts and helping them develop self-esteem.

"If students think they are nothing, I say, 'You are marvelous. Never forget me, a teacher who sees who you are and loves you, no matter what your grades are.' I want every student to feel they are the only one in this teacher's life."

Her husband's father was a well-known professor. Dr. David Flusser, one of the world's foremost Jewish authorities on the New Testament and early Christianity, wrote a biography of Jesus.

Flusser won the prestigious Israel Prize for literature in 1980. Ironically, after traveling to India once to lecture, the native of Vienna, Austria, came back to Israel and told his 4-year-old son, Johanan, it would be good for him to marry an Indian woman someday.

The father's wish came true when Johanan met Miri at a Jerusalem book fair while she was in college. She immediately knew that this was the man she wanted to marry, because he was religious, open, smart and kind.

Two weeks after their wedding, Miri and Johanan went to live in Switzerland for 10 months while he pursued the scientific study of animal behavior at Zurich University. "It was wonderful. It was a 10-month honeymoon," reflects Miri.

Now she dreams of seeing India, her other homeland. At 51, Miri is embracing the Indian part of her rich heritage – in addition to her Israeli part – as never before. "I understand that I am an Indian woman. I'm also an Israeli woman. Inside, I'm Indian. I always thought I was different. I'm a mystical woman; I understand things that people generally don't understand."

For Miri, every day is like Yom Kippur, the Day of Atonement. She takes personal inventory to see where she can improve her character and relations with God, herself and other people.

She focuses on fulfilling her purpose in this lifetime. One thing she knows for sure: "It's not to come here and enjoy. You have a duty." For her soul, that has included teaching thousands of children. In the second half of her life, that may expand to counseling adults, giving them the benefit of her inner work and personal exploration.

As much as Miri would like to travel the world, her feet remain firmly planted in Israel. "Here, I speak Hebrew, I read Hebrew. I can be religious in my way. This is my home.

"Our family is an example of the beauty and uniqueness of this country. I came from India, and my husband came from Czechoslovakia and Germany. Two worlds, east and west, came together. He brings classical music; I like Israeli music. We blend traditions from here, traditions from there. For me, wow, it's wonderful.

"People come from all over the world. Jews here can be religious if they choose. We were in Switzerland, and while it was so beautiful, it was very hard for me. I felt like a foreigner. I am black; Johanan is white. I suffered. Here in Israel, I feel comfortable.

"I'm happy to be Israeli – but from India."

Chana Bracha Siegelbaum

Founder And Director Of
Midreshet B'erot Bat Ayin
Born 1960, Copenhagen, Denmark

Chana Bracha Siegelbaum

In Israel I Feel My Soul Vibrating

My rabbi lives in Bat Ayin, a funky Jewish village in
the scenic Judean hills near Jerusalem. We met when he
had a pulpit in my hometown of Knoxville, Tennessee,
a conservative American city in the foothills of the lush
Smoky Mountains. The two places are worlds apart,
but Yehoshua Kahan connects them for me.

He also connected me with Chana Bracha
Siegelbaum, his eclectic next-door neighbor in Bat Ayin.
She is a former flower child from Denmark who found
her soul, her husband and her calling in Israel. Now
a rebbetzin, or rabbi's wife, Chana Bracha started
a Jewish studies program for women that integrates
the Jewish Bible and spirituality with creativity and
environmental awareness.

The Kahans and the Siegelbaums are among some
130 families – comprising rabbis and Torah scholars,
artists and musicians, nutritionists and holistic healers,
meditation teachers and movement therapists – who
populate Bat Ayin – Hebrew for "Daughter of the Eye."
They overlook sweeping vistas of Israel. They also tend
to see the world differently from the mainstream.

When I meet Chana Bracha one November morning,

she wants to keep gardening while we talk so as not to waste precious, limited time. Flies buzz around her as she digs hands deep into the soil, planting artichokes and picking radishes and edible weeds called malva. The unconventional interview setting reflects her colorful spirit.

How Chana Bracha Siegelbaum made her way from Copenhagen, Denmark, home of the Little Mermaid statue and Tivoli Gardens fairy tale amusement park, to Bat Ayin, Israel, a village of rugged homes and dusty, boulder-strewn roads, is a story straight out of the 1960s. It concerns hippie culture, rebellion against Western values, and spiritual seeking.

For Chana Bracha, a spiritual healer and founder of a women's seminary, it was a journey to explore the unknown world of her Jewish heritage.

As she says, "The truth is that, although I grew up in an assimilated secular home, I seem to have been born religious. My religiosity was not expressed through any conscious observance of Jewish laws or rituals; yet, as far back as I can recall, I remember praying to God every night. It felt quite natural to address Him every night: my own secret comforter, who was always there for me."

Chana Bracha was born in Denmark in 1960, the granddaughter of a Hasidic yeshiva (school for learning traditional Jewish texts) student captivated by the secular enlightenment. Ironically, she returned to the place he left behind. "As I entered seventh grade, I began to question all the values of the society in which I had been raised. The Judaism to which I had been exposed seemed like an empty, hypocritical religion."

In high school, Chana Bracha found expression as a hippie wearing flowing Indian tunics and flowers in her hair. In the classrooms, she insisted on sitting on a little rug on the floor.

Following a fashion of the era, she and her friends sought to expand their consciousness and enter a brave new world, practicing yoga and meditation and reading the likes of Aldous Huxley, Carlos Castaneda and Hermann Hesse.

After graduation, she set out to explore the world beyond Denmark, traveling lightly with a backpack and outstretched thumb. The idealistic young woman with clear blue eyes hitchhiked through Europe but soon ran out of money and courage. She phoned home from Paris, and her parents wired her a ticket to Israel, where relatives lived. She had found solace when visiting family in the Promised Land before.

"In Israel I feel my soul vibrating. Any other place in the world, I never felt alive. I felt some part of my life was not activated."

The energy and sanctity of the Western Wall pierced her soul. A stranger named Chava invited her for tea in the Old City of Jerusalem. When Chava shared spiritual insights she had learned in the women's division of Diaspora Yeshiva where she studied Judaism, Chana Bracha found herself deeply moved. She had a sense that here was a friend who could share her quest for truth. The very next day, during the summer of 1979, she enrolled in the yeshiva and began to open her heart to the religion of her ancestors. At the yeshiva, she uncovered the vibrancy of Judaism through singing, dancing, prayer and community.

Now as Rebbetzin Chana Bracha, she is able to pass on the fruits of her search to a new generation of young women on their own spiritual quest. They often pause at a crossroads in their lives and come to Bat Ayin thirsting for answers. Representing all ages, nationalities and religious backgrounds, they learn and grow at a women's seminary called Midreshet B'erot Bat Ayin, which Chana Bracha founded in 1996. B'erot, which means wellsprings, is designed to nourish their souls with intense Torah learning and a lifestyle to match.

"Midreshet B'erot Bat Ayin encompasses a central part

of my life," says Chana Bracha as she tends her garden. "I founded the school because there wasn't any place where a woman could learn Torah and express her creativity." For her, environmental consciousness is part of the Torah. She weaves herbology, nutrition and health into her lessons. Her organic garden, which includes arugula and strawberries, sits on a half-acre with a variety of fruit trees, from apples to apricots and plums to pomegranates. Leafy greens are in abundant supply for Sabbath meals. Chana Bracha models the mitzva, or good deed, of waste preservation by turning leftover food into compost or chicken feed.

"Torah teaches you have to be healthy and eat healthy. The importance of connecting with nature and the environment are part of the Torah as well, but a lot of people don't know it.

"God created us. We have to be grateful for the gift of life."

In addition to the staples – classes in Jewish texts – B'erot offers art, music, dance, drama, Jewish meditation, health and nutrition, and agricultural workshops. Chana Bracha says her mission is to engage the whole student – mind, body and soul – through a curriculum that combines academic Torah learning with innovative classes and workshops. She also wants students to deepen their connection to the land of Israel while tapping into the hidden feminine power of the universe to better the world.

A personal commitment drives Chana Bracha. She lives what she teaches, even down to signing her correspondence, "With blessings of the Torah and the Land."

The road to claiming the Torah and the Land for herself started in Denmark, ran through Israel, then detoured in Memphis, Tennessee, where her American-born husband paid back his medical school scholarship by working as a prison doctor. After their return to Israel, he became an emergency room physician in Jerusalem. The couple have two sons and two granddaughters.

The Siegelbaums met one Sabbath as students in the Old City of Jerusalem. After a Sabbath meal at the home of mutual friends, her husband-to-be walked Chana Bracha back to her dormitory. Thus began a ritual of taking daily walks together all over the Old City. "We became familiar with every single arch and winding gateway, as we explored the road to each other's heart. After having been at yeshiva only five months, we announced our engagement. We were one of the many couples who were married under the beautiful wedding canopy with the symbols of the 12 tribes, hand-woven by some of the women in the yeshiva."

They have made their home in Bat Ayin since 1992. The couple lived in a caravan – what Americans would call a mobile home – before settling in a house with a yard, fruit trees, garden and expansive view of the Judean hills.

"People here believe in the importance of growing the land. It's a very diverse community of people. You don't have to be one stream of Judaism. For people who are already Orthodox, it feels very good and accepting that you don't have to be one stream."

Bat Ayin residents tend to share the same ideals and philosophy of life, she adds. They want to serve God and like to delve into Jewish mysticism. Prayer is an important and soulful expression of their beliefs.

Chana Bracha believes her path is to help repair the world by living in harmony with the land of Israel and learning Torah. She delights in questioning and growing, and nurturing that process in others. The young women of Midreshet B'erot Bat Ayin who look to her for guidance help keep Chana Bracha's spiritual light burning brightly. Meanwhile, the land of Israel keeps her soul vibrating.

Faydra Shapiro

Professor, Founder Of The Selah Workshop
Born 1970, Toronto, Canada

Faydra Shapiro

Connecting Christians With The People Of Israel

I'm sitting at a picnic table on a windswept hill in the Galilee this Friday morning, animatedly chatting with a 39-year-old Orthodox woman who feels like a kindred spirit. Dr. Faydra Shapiro grew up in an assimilated Jewish family in Canada; I grew up in an assimilated Jewish family in the South of the United States. She had become interested in evangelical Christians as a university professor; my life had intersected with them ever since childhood in Tennessee.

Both of our lives had been touched by Yehoshua Kahan, formerly rabbi of my synagogue in Tennessee and later Faydra's teacher at Livnot U'Lehibanot, a program in Tsfat, or Safed. He had recommended her as a dynamic personality for me to interview because of her passion for showing Christians the personal side of the Holy Land. A professor of religion, Faydra founded The Selah Workshop to connect Christian groups with the people of Israel in the Land of Israel.

I took the 6:45 a.m. bus for a two-hour ride from Jerusalem to the Golani Junction, a major crossroads in the Galilee, to meet her – and was not disappointed. Faydra blends zeal for her dream of teaching Christian

78

visitors about Israel with a solid academic background and personal warmth. She not only had met me at the bus stop five minutes from her house, but also had given a lift to two young women who needed transportation to her idyllic community of Mitzpe Netofa.

Faydra's Israeli-born husband, Shaul, extended hospitality as well, bringing us apples and hot tea as we schmoozed on an overlook by a synagogue near their house. It was the perfect setting for talking about Faydra's journey from city life in Toronto to caravilla in the Galilee.

F aydra Shapiro first visited Israel for her bat mitzva. The trip planted a seed that kept growing. She graduated high school in Toronto, Canada, in 1988, then studied in Livnot U'Lehibanot, a program in Tsfat, also known as Safed, geared toward young Jews with little or no background in Judaism. The name is Hebrew for "to build and to be built," referring to the contribution the participants make to the Land of Israel and to their own knowledge base.

Livnot became a foundation for Faydra's life. She went back to Israel as often as possible, returning as a staff member and to do graduate school research that became her first book, "Building Jewish Roots: The Israel Experience."

In it, Faydra explores how Israel experience programs like Livnot help mostly unaffiliated participants in their 20s create rich and varied Jewish identities.

The seeds bore fruit for her. Many visits later, Faydra came back with her Israeli-born husband, Shaul Katzenstein, and their five young children, whose ages cover a span of seven years. She became a citizen of Israel in August 2008.

"Once upon a time, I had a normal life," jokes Faydra, clad in a bright orange, long-sleeved shirt, blue jean skirt and black tichel, a headscarf worn by married Jewish women who are religious.

"I had a house, and I had a career, and it was going swimmingly. I had a tenured position at a Canadian university. I had this book, and I had a book award. I had a research grant, and I'm at the height of my career. And all of a sudden, there's this new focus, this new vision."

Her husband had always wanted to return to Israel, ever since he went to college in Canada. They met as students at McMaster University when Faydra was nearing the end of her doctoral work in religious studies and he was a new student in the program.

By the time they married in 1999, Faydra already had started teaching in the Department of Religion and Culture at Wilfrid Laurier. She earned her doctorate degree in 2000, had her first child in 2001, received tenure from the university in 2005, then published "Building Jewish Roots" and won a National Jewish Book Award in 2006.

The family took a sabbatical year in Jerusalem from 2006 to 2007 so that she could work on her next research project, in which she examined Christian Zionism.

As Faydra explains, "I was hearing about Christians who loved Jews and Israel. I started meeting with people and reading and finding out a little bit more. It was so out of the ordinary for me. I found they were interested in Judaism, they were positive and encouraging, and they were extremely knowledgeable about Israel. It didn't fit my stereotypes about who evangelicals were. So I proposed that for my research project."

Faydra's plan to take a year off in Israel and then return to normal life in Canada got derailed. "What happened was I started chasing these Christians around with my tape recorder and kind of got inspired along the way. I was hearing from them about the beauty of Jews living in Israel and about Jews and Christians reading the Bible and taking it seriously. Something happened. It's like a switch flipped.

"By the middle of that year, it was very clear to us this

was where we needed to be. I watched my children blossom. It was good for me. It was good for my husband. We went back to Canada and prepared for aliya (moving to Israel)."

It took a year to prepare on many levels, including emotionally and materially. Faydra realized that she had stopped being afraid – of what would become of her career, of the adjustment to a new culture, and of financial insecurity. She felt liberated and eager.

"I sort of drank the aliya Kool-Aid. Suddenly, it was doable for me."

Having scoped out several communities during the sabbatical year, the family settled on Mitzpe Netofa, which means lookout of the Beit Netofa Valley. The Lower Galilee community of about 130 families weds religious Jews from various backgrounds, including American, Australian, Belgian, British, Canadian, French, German, Israeli, Moroccan, Russian, South African, Tunisian and Yemenite.

The neighbors welcomed them with open arms. "Our arrival was incredible," says Faydra, recalling signs on the door, sheets on the bed and food in the refrigerator, not to mention assistance carrying in luggage, cooking meals and keeping the children occupied.

The community also helped them enroll their children in school and make connections for jobs.

Faydra and Shaul rented a four-bedroom, two-bath "caravilla," temporary quarters where the new immigrants could see if the community felt right for them.

"It's a comfortable place for Jews from North America to land. It's a safe environment. We grew up in big cities, so this is a major lifestyle change. You have a year or two to get adjusted to life in a small community and see if it's really right for you and do it in a supportive environment."

She also considers Mitzpe Netofa a wholesome environment where children have room to run and play outdoors. "In North America, you overparent, wondering whose house is my kid at.

Here, you know they're probably at so-and-so's house and they'll come home when it's dark."

Nestled amid olive trees, forests and farms, Faydra's new home is conveniently located for her Selah workshops to teach Christian tourists about the land, people and culture of Israel.

"In terms of Christian sites, this is the heart of it," says Faydra, whose name comes from Greek mythology. "We're 20 minutes from Nazareth and an hour from Capernaum."

Selah brings Israel to life beyond the traditional holy sites; it emphasizes genuine connection with Israelis. Faydra realized the question of what to offer repeat Christian tourists was not being answered. Thus, she put together nature hikes in the Golan and Galilee, classes on topics like the Hebrew Bible and Jewish family values, Sabbath meals with Israeli families, and volunteer opportunities such as visiting the elderly and serving children with special needs. Her groups can see the land of milk and honey in action by picking dates or making their own olive oil.

"People still should be taking the standard travel agent tour of Israel," Faydra suggests. "We are seeking to add to it. Many Christian visitors come to Israel a lot. How do we keep that vitally important group of people connected and engaging with Israel? They have to be rooted in the country; they have to know people. What does it mean to be an 18-year-old soldier, a new immigrant or a farmer?"

In her experience, evangelical Christians want to engage in the modern-day miracle of Israel that for them is evidence God is faithful to His word.

With Faydra's specialty in contemporary evangelical-Jewish relations, she dreams of opening an academic center for that kind of study at an Israeli university. In the meantime, she still travels often to Canada to maintain her teaching and university responsibilities.

Christian Zionists represent a vital segment of the North American population, she says, because they can speak in an articulate manner about the reality of life in Israel that goes beyond stereotypes about warfare and racism.

"They can see it's all shades of gray here. They can bring that message home to their churches and communities and pass along the truth that isn't filtered through the media."

Her groups of pro-Israel evangelicals come from other parts of the world as well, from France to Nigeria to South Africa. They sometimes attempt to missionize Faydra, which does not surprise or offend her.

"My way to handle it is to turn it into an engagement. To engage is to participate in something. When you engage an idea is when you wrestle with it. I may totally disagree, but we're talking. I can hear your narrative and say, 'Thank you very much.'

"Real relationships are about saying the unsaid. It's not about painting over the differences, but putting them on the table. Now what can we do about those differences?"

Faydra appreciates the opportunity to serve as a bridge between worlds. The professor's training in religious studies gives her a facility to put issues into historical context.

She tells Selah participants, "Don't worry about offending me. Go ahead and ask. Don't worry about getting it right."

Their enthusiasm and curiosity inspire her. She says yesterday, for instance, "I had people hugging me and crying. I think to be able to tell our stories in a safe, honest environment has an effect on people. Because they don't know how to ask and who to ask. They really want to know."

In the same spirit of openness, Faydra wants her children to be able to engage with the world and not avoid others who are different. She conveys this by example – for instance, teaching English in the Arab village next door.

"The Jewish and the Arab sectors in Israel just don't meet, for the most part. So to be standing there as a Jewish lady – we're not doing interfaith dialogue; we're not talking politics; we're just doing skills. They laugh at my pronunciation of their Arabic names. It's making people people."

Likewise, Ali, an Arab from the neighboring village, teaches karate to her children in Mitzpe Netofa.

"That's not going to make peace, but it gives people personal experiences of each other. I think these kinds of relationships show there are a lot of good people in the world."

Moshe Basson

Restaurateur – Chef
Born 1950, Amarah, Iraq

Moshe Basson

Spicing Biblical Cooking With Torah

My cousins met some colorful characters, or "Jerusalem personalities," on a Wexner Heritage Program Israel Institute tour one summer. That's how I came to learn of Moshe Basson. The swarthy, ponytailed chef entertains visiting dignitaries with his Biblical cooking and "Land of Israel" food.

Born in Iraq in 1950, Moshe has spiced up the culinary scene of the Holy Land for decades. I was delighted to first sample the dinner fare at his Eucalyptus restaurant when it was located in the Russian Compound of Jerusalem, beginning with tamarind juice and ending with tehina date honey cake and wine.

As luck would have it, a tour group of Christian journalists from Canada also visited Eucalyptus that night. I joined their table and enjoyed the North American camaraderie as Moshe regaled us with stories of food from the old country – ancient Israel.

After they parted, I sat in the back dining room with Moshe and interviewed him as he dined on chicken from his kitchen. He then kindly offered to drive me home in his sputtering old car. Fortunately, my friends' apartment was on his way – and as I was at the end of

my stay, with my flight returning to the United States
the next day, I had few shekels left for a cab.

Moshe Basson's life is an exotic stew. The ingredients include Iraqi roots, an Israeli upbringing and a multicultural outlook as a member of Chefs for Peace.

The co-owner of Jerusalem's Eucalyptus restaurant, he has molded his career as a chef with a specialty in Biblical cooking spiced with hyssop, mallow, sage and sumac. His "Land of Israel" dishes showcase Mediterranean delights such as Jerusalem artichokes, tehina, couscous and carob, and the seven species – barley, wheat, dates, figs, olives, grapes and pomegranates.

Moshe blends kitchen artistry and Torah, braiding together modern food dishes and ancient Biblical references. He points to a plate of spices and notes that hyssop played a leading part in the 10th plague before the exodus from Egypt. The Jews used hyssop to paint lamb's blood on their doorposts, thereby marking their homes so the angel of death would pass over them and not take their firstborn sons.

Entertaining a group of North American journalists who are beginning their meal with red lentil soup, Moshe invokes a story in Genesis. He recalls how Jacob enticed twin brother Esau, who came out of the womb red all over, to sell his birthright for a pot of hearty lentil stew. A journalist asks, tongue in cheek, if his tablemates will receive a blessing if they eat the soup.

Moshe heard Biblical stories from his father, a baker. The chef, wearing his hair in a long braid, defines himself as a traditional Jew who believes in God and the Bible. Born in Iraq in 1950, he came to Israel as a baby when his family immigrated and became citizens.

"We left everything behind us. The situation of the Jewish people in Arab countries became very bad. It wasn't easy to leave 2,000 years of tradition, but it was impossible to stay there.

People were pushed out. They took away the citizenship of the family, as far as I know."

Each person leaving Iraq was allowed to take one suitcase and a ring. Moshe's resourceful grandfather had crafted hidden flaps in their shoes for transporting gold. The family began their new life in an aluminum shed with one window and one door in a Jerusalem-area refugee camp. As Moshe says, "If you were lucky, there was cement under your feet."

The young Iraqi-Israeli grew up in the Jewish tradition of the east. At age 8, he started experimenting with cooking, which was only natural, considering his lineage.

"The intoxicating aroma of lentil stew takes me to the Arab village of Beit Safafa near Jerusalem to our family bakery in the 1960s," Moshe recounts in the 2008 "Slow Food Almanac." "I'm a little boy, and this time the aroma is that of shourbat aadds, an Arab lentil soup that Zeinab, our Arab neighbor, cooks. Zeinab is like an aunt for me. ... And like Moses who sees the Promised Land but cannot enter, I see, smell and feel. I can even hear the foods and savory dishes as my Auntie Zeinab prepares them, but I cannot consume them. Those savory dishes cooked in a separate stove in my father's bakery are not kosher, which means I cannot eat them. Though, I'm allowed to fantasize."

The 1960s were not so innocent, however. Moshe recalls seeing fear reflected in the eyes of the adults. He relates how his family, terrified of being bombed, glued shut the windows of their home during the Six-Day War between Israel and neighboring states Egypt, Jordan and Syria in June 1967. They used sacks of soil to fortify the entrance against intruders.

Since the 1970s, Moshe has heeded the call of his soul to create food with Biblical roots. He picks herbs and spices in the Jerusalem hills and fruits and vegetables in the Machane Yehuda open-air market downtown.

His father used to make mountains of colorful Iraqi-Jewish traditional sweets, dripping with honey, to transport to the shuk, or market. The family had a tradition of hundreds of years making sweets in Moshe's birthplace in Amarah, between the Tigris and Euphrates rivers in Iraq – the Biblical Babel.

Moshe's tongues include Arabic, French, English, Italian and Spanish, in addition to Iraqi and Hebrew. He calls his couscous manna di cielo, Italian for manna from heaven. In 2006, Italy's president knighted him for reviving Biblical food. As an example, Moshe uses a family recipe to make Gersh carmel, recreating a dish he says King David carried onto the battlefield with Goliath.

"At my place, the tradition of my Jewish ancestors since the days of the prophets and the kings blends with the tradition of Palestine Arab cooking and the Iraqi origins of my family," Moshe writes in "Slow Food Almanac."

A member of the Chefs for Peace association of Israeli Jews, Christians and Muslims, he feels a spiritual connection with others through cooking. The table is like an altar, and food and words of Torah, his offering. Moshe muses about such a melange: "It's like Someone puts the answer in your mouth."

He prays daily – not formulated prayers, but personal dialogue. "I'm talking with my Lord, my Father. It's a conversation." From time to time, that unfolds in a synagogue.

Moshe, still in his white chef's coat and blue jeans, eats a bite after the restaurant clears. He talks about the importance of relating one's story. "V'higadita l'bincha – And you should tell your son. We're not telling our children why we are here in Israel. Tell your son what happened when you came from Iraq as a refugee."

He has three children: Ronny, a cook like his dad; Sharon, a baker; and Lior, who works in high technology and also makes dynamite pasta sauce. Moshe is intent on preserving their heritage through his cooking and food narrative. Meanwhile, he also serves the world. Over the years, he has fed foreign dignitaries, Israeli cabinet ministers and homeless persons alike.

In 2004, Moshe and his partner, Rabbi Yehuda Azrad, created an eatery catering to different classes and tastes. Carmei

Ha'ir (Vineyards of the City), their restaurant in the open-air market of downtown Jerusalem, would provide food with dignity, offering a choice of entrees, table service and a restaurant atmosphere.

Moshe put his gourmet spin on simple home cooking, for instance, spicing up lentil soup with lemon, garlic, cilantro, coriander and cumin.

He aimed to reach not only the longtime poor, but also the newly poor Israelis who had lost their businesses or jobs because of a faltering economy. He empathized with the latter, having faced financial difficulties at Eucalyptus when it was located on Jaffa Road, where suicide bombers struck repeatedly and drove customers away.

"I wanted to reach people experiencing poverty for the first time. ... Sometimes, they are the most poor because they aren't accepting assistance from anyone. They haven't raised the white flag. If the place has the stigma of a soup kitchen, these people will never go in. In our society, people don't die from hunger; they die from shame," Moshe told The Christian Science Monitor.

The concept was novel: Only those with money would pay for their meals – whatever amount they decided. Supporters in Israel and other countries helped with the restaurant's expenses. But the demand for free meals proved greater than expected, and the restaurant struggled.

Still, Moshe simmered with passion about the concept. He refers to the Deuteronomy verse that says, "Every man shall bring according to the ability of his hand to give." Give as you are able. He liked the egalitarian service by volunteer waiters. "Whether you are a judge, doctor, lawyer or not, everybody is treated the same."

Whether at the fancy Eucalyptus or the modest Carmei Ha'ir, Moshe could be counted on to dish up idealism with his Biblical food and Torah.

Lev Strinkovsky

Violin-Maker
Born 1950, Baku, Former Soviet Union

Lev Strinkovsky

Taking A Bow

After making aliya, or becoming an Israeli citizen, in 1999, I lived on a narrow, one-way street in the Katamon neighborhood of Jerusalem, near the president's residence and an Islamic art museum. Around the corner from my apartment sat Russian-born violin-maker Lev Strinkovsky's modest shop. A small wooden violin scroll on the sign outside his door intrigued me, and we talked one day. I learned he practiced an unusual old-time craft and had a fine sense of humor. He eventually became a "slice of life" subject for a Jerusalem Post article, in which I called him a "teddy bear of a guy from the former Soviet Union."

Ten years later, I found Lev still conducting business in his workshop on Rehov Haportzim, making, selling and repairing string and bow instruments. Wearing a black T-shirt and jeans, he was still low-key, kind and very funny, especially when telling jokes about the motherland. For instance: After the Russian Revolution, people asked a journalist what had changed. The journalist told them to ask his dog. They did, and the dog dryly replied, "My chain is a little bit longer. They *put my food a little farther away. But I can bark as much as I want."*

In Israel, by contrast, Lev has enjoyed a long leash. That includes the freedom to travel – in fact, he and his family had just driven to Italy and Switzerland. "My life is quite comfortable," he reflects. "I'm working. We can make a living. There are a lot of things that make me nervous, but there is no ideal place on earth – not here, not Russia, America, Canada, Australia, anywhere."

Lev Strinkovsky could have stayed in Baku, Azerbaijan, and hit the high notes of his career as a violinist. But instead, the established musician chose to move to Israel in 1979 and start from the ground up as a violin-maker.

His mother decided when he was born that he would become a violinist. She had studied violin at the Stolarsky Music School in Odessa until age 14, when war erupted in what was then the Soviet Union. Many Jewish families, including hers, fled from the Nazis.

Hers ended up in Stalingrad, which endured the coldest winter anyone could remember in 100 years. She suffered frostbite, damaging her fingers and ending her musical career. Lev, her elder son, would live out her dreams.

"She decided I had to continue her career of playing violin. I started as well playing violin at age 7," he says one rainy November morning before customers begin to trickle into his shop. Violins, violas, cellos, guitars and a balalaika line the walls and cases behind him.

Lev studied throughout high school, college and government music academy in Azerbaijan. He earned a master's degree in violin and viola performance and teaching, played with the philharmonic, radio city and Staatsorchestra, and toured the country.

His mother was happy, but Lev was not. Despite his talent,

he did not want to be a musician. "I was really good. But I like this profession much more," says the violin-maker. "You cannot do two things well at the same time. Music you have to practice every day two to three hours. You have concerts. You have to be in good shape all the time. It's like a sport. You can't leave it and then come back."

The same could be said of the motherland. He left the familiar trappings of the former Soviet Union and found a new life and calling in Israel. The Strinkovsky family's drama illustrated the struggle for the rights of Soviet Jews in the 1970s and 1980s. Life was harsh in the totalitarian country – particularly for those who spearheaded a movement for their personal and collective dignity as Jews and their right to immigrate to Israel.

Lev's father, Israel, managed a government fur factory. Because of the high demand for fur, Russians called it "soft gold." The government made a case of some bureaucratic problems, tried Israel for them, and sent him to jail for four years. Details of the charges were sketchy, according to Lev: "I don't know what happened, but it was a difficult time for our family."

It took seven years for the entire Strinkovsky family – parents, two brothers and their spouses and children – to be able to immigrate to Israel. Behind the Iron Curtain, more mysterious problems arose.

As Lev explains, "You had to refuse officially your citizenship to leave the Soviet Union. For a Soviet citizen, it was a shame to tell the government, 'I want to leave.' It looked bad for Russia before the 1980 Olympics. At that time, the government took your passport if you were making aliya and gave you a visa for two months. They gave you your paper with a photo. This was your document for everything. If you didn't finish your arrangements in two months, they didn't care. I had three days left to finish my visa, and realized they had lost our lift." The family's shipment of household belongings had not left yet for Israel.

Officials told Lev they would extend the visa for only three more days so he could track down the lift. They said his family could go on and he would stay in jail if his visa ran out. At the last minute, he cracked the case through documents and telephone calls. The lift had been sent by mistake to a station 300 miles from Moscow. Fortunately, Lev was able to iron out the mess in time and fly with his family to Vienna, Austria, as planned, and then on to Israel. They left behind frigid temperatures of 45 degrees below in Moscow and arrived at Ben-Gurion Airport on Feb. 25, 1979.

"We were lucky because they wanted to let us go quickly before the Olympic Games, but they made a lot of trouble just for the sake of making trouble."

Much has changed since those days of struggle for the rights of Soviet Jews in the 1970s and 1980s. Close to 1 million Russian-speaking immigrants live in Israel, although one-third of them are not Jewish by the standards of Orthodox Jewish law.

"The Jewish Agency told me, 'You are a violinist; OK, there is a chamber orchestra in Beersheba. Go there.'" The government also needed teachers there in the Negev Desert. Lev taught music, and his wife, Esther, taught English. The politics of making aliya were different then, he says.

"Now, you can choose anyplace in Israel; if you have relatives who can take you for a few days or weeks, you can go there. At that time, you could not do that. They wanted to put you where they wanted to put you. So we went to a mercaz klita (absorption center) in Beersheba for four months. I started work as a night guard at a mental hospital. After two to three weeks, they put me in the position of night clerk because I spoke Hebrew well.

"Our teacher, Jacqueline, was a Moroccan Jewish woman. Our group was all people from the Soviet Union. She told us she hadn't had such an advanced group in many years. She told me, 'You are the best of my pupils in my career.' I have a very good ear. I catch Hebrew, English and French from the air. I am very stupid in mathematics or something like that. My brother was very talented in mathematics and physics. I have two things: the languages, and I can make anything from nothing."

Trained from a young age to listen to and remember music, he translates that skill into learning languages, and speaks English, French, Hebrew and Turkish in addition to his native Russian.

The Strinkovskys left the absorption center after a few months and moved to Jerusalem, where Esther had landed a position at Bank Leumi. Lev had made the acquaintance of a violin-maker named Joseph Boazson, whose sensibilities struck a chord with him. "He was a very, very good violin-maker. I told him I was a professional violin player. He asked if I knew how to do repairs. He was looking for an assistant."

So Lev, whose name is Hebrew for "heart," started making violins at age 28 as an apprentice to Boazson. After years of working on a bench in his home, Lev opened his own shop in 1984. "I like it very, very much. It's my life," he says, although he is also the very proud father of two girls.

His specialty is making violins, violas and cellos, and repairing all stringed instruments except pianos. While pint-size violins, complete with case and red bow, begin at around $150, the adult versions start at around $200. Lev makes violas – even cellos – by special order. "The wood is expensive. With the material you spend on one cello, you can make four violins."

He serves music academy students, teachers, amateurs, orchestra members and concertmasters from Tel-Aviv to Eilat. Walk-in patrons range from a Hasid who wants new hair on his bow to a woman who needs a string fixed on her cello.

Lev meets the small and the great. He makes tiny violins – beginning at 1/16 size – for tots. He has repaired the violin and bow of Russian-born, American violinist Isaac Stern, whose signed photo graces the wall, along with one of Mstislav Rostropovich, a fellow Baku native. Rostropovich, the late cellist, Washington, D.C., symphony orchestra conductor and humanitarian, was driven to exile in his homeland after sheltering and supporting dissidents.

Born in 1950, the gray-haired Lev has crossed paths with

many famous names from that era of Soviet history. He played concerts with Rostropovich in the former Soviet Union.

"He tried my cello, and he was very, very pleased. The feedback was very good," Lev recalls of a meeting with Rostropovich in Baku. He and his colleagues toured with the famous cellist.

In her job at the Israel Ministry of Absorption, Lev's wife has worked with one of the world's most recognized "refuseniks," Natan Sharansky, who served in a prison camp in the Siberian gulag and became a symbol for human rights and Soviet Jewry.

Lev also is a product of his era. He says when he was growing up in the former Soviet Union, "We were brainwashed to believe there is no God and religion is a mistake. We are not religious at all. This is part of our Soviet Union behavior. We are atheist. But not only us; a lot of people here."

Although he and Esther have lived in Israel for more than three decades, they still remain hybrids. As Lev says, laughing, "Our culture, behavior, mentality and point of view are different. We are not here, but we are not there. We are in between."

Sam Greene

Born Glasgow, Scotland
1905 – 2008

Sam Greene

Great Scot: Sharp Memory And Wit At 102

Ronah Lewis and her husband, Srul, pick me up at the bus stop in sunny Herzliya in their little Toyota Yaris. We're going to meet her dad, a 101 1/2-year-old Scotsman, at the golden-age home where he resides. His first 100 years, Samuel Greene lived independently. Then he moved to Beth Protea, a senior citizen facility founded by the Southern African community in Israel and worldwide. This isn't like any retirement home I've seen in the United States. It's vibrant. People sit in the upstairs lobby discussing Israeli politics and the philharmonic. With a synagogue, indoor pool, library and lounge, there's plenty to do here.

We find Sam Greene holding court downstairs by the kosher dining room. His remarkable memory and wry sense of humor draw friends and family to him.

Sam Greene was born in Glasgow, Scotland, in 1905. "I remember there was always a car or two because my father had a Model T. There was very little traffic at that time," he relates.

His parents, who came from White Russia, had relatives in Scotland. The population in Glasgow was around 1 million when Sam was young. "At one time, I reckon, in my early days there were 17,000 or 18,000 Jews in Glasgow. This is where they united at one time."

The Greenes and their 10 children lived in the Jewish district of Gorbals. Sam's father helped start a synagogue called Chevra Kadisha (Holy Society).

"We weren't very Orthodox, but we did keep Shabbat," Sam says, his memories from a century ago in sharp focus. "Jewish life there was quite a good life. There were very few people who were rich. The norm was poverty. When I say poverty, it wasn't a bad feeling to be poor. Everybody else was poor. The poor who help the poor."

Those who managed to succeed financially left the Gorbals to create a better lifestyle for themselves and their families.

Sam served with the British Air Force, and received the Burma Star. "The thing being," he explains, "I was sent off to India and was in the Royal Air Force regiment. Then I did a certain amount of time with them." It added up to a total of three years in India and Burma.

He adds some dry Scotch humor: "I've a good record. I've never fought. I've never been defeated.

"The only fighting I did was, if I knew the enemy was over there, I went the other way. I have been in a campaign or two, but it's not worth mentioning."

As his daughter, Ronah, says later, he's an incredibly modest man.

Ronah is one of Sam's three children, all born in Darlington, England. Sam fell in love with an Englishwoman, Phyliss, and married her in 1937. That's how he came to leave Scotland. After retiring from the service with his Burma Star, he set up a gents and youth outfitters shop in Darlington. He had the franchise for Levi's there.

Two daughters moved to Israel as young adults, and Sam and his wife visited them and their families often. He admits, "I can't speak Hebrew. I can understand a word or two. I think I can speak Yiddish very well, and I can understand it better."

So in later years when his wife became ill, it made sense for Sam and her to move to Israel to be near their brood. He made aliya – became a citizen – at age 80.

"I didn't come here to work, as you can understand. The thing being, my wife wasn't too well. I thought I'd better get going, because my children wanted us to come to Israel. I don't suppose if they'd remained in England, we'd have come here."

Ronah remembers her parents had been living in Israel only a few months in 1985 when tensions escalated with Lebanon. Friends from Darlington begged them to come back. They chose to stay.

"This was something I intended to go through with, the aliya," Sam declares. "First of all, it's a Jewish country. I like the Jewish people."

Even though he's not religious, Ronah says, her father has a deeply Jewish soul.

His beloved wife passed away in 1995, and Sam lived on his own until he reached 100. The Scot-Israeli claims no secrets to his longevity, although, he allows, "I did like a glass of whiskey at one time."

Ronah attributes his vitality to good genes. "I think he's a remarkable man, not so much what he's done, but what he is now," she says proudly.

People enjoy Sam's company, as evidenced this Friday morning. He receives many visitors, including his daughters, their husbands, two grandchildren, three great-grandchildren, family friends, newfound admirers, and staff members at Beth Protea.

Ronah reports, "All the people that come love to visit him. He doesn't make a lot of fuss. He used to make a lot of jokes. He remembers stories."

For his part, Sam says his life is going on here in the Herzliya golden-age home. He still walks, enjoys his family and friends, and takes pleasure in eating.

"I think he's amazing. He still has his dignity," Ronah says. "I have this wonderful man sitting there I can discuss things with – like what's going on in the world."

Joe & Marion Goodstein

Homemaker
Marion – Born 1929, Birmingham, Alabama

Architect
Joe – Born 1925, Knoxville, Tennessee

Joe & Marion Goodstein

Shalom, Y'all ... The Long Goodbye

The 1960s house with the butterfly roof and orange door they had built and lived in for 42 years languished on the market for a long time. I secretly hoped it wouldn't sell and they would change their minds about leaving. She taught me Hebrew and the art of baking challa, the braided bread eaten on the Sabbath and Jewish holidays. I sat with them in services, year after year, learning when to rise, when to sit and when to bow. They made me an honorary member of their family – along with hundreds of others who graced their Sabbath and holiday table. They even let my old dog, Scamp, come with me when he became too fearful to stay alone at night.

I would miss them too much. Life wouldn't be the same without them in our little Jewish community. Maybe they would give up and downsize to a condominium after all.

Then it happened. They had a real offer on the house, and the two-year-long goodbye suddenly had an ending in sight. They were packing up their 5,000-square-foot home and moving to a 900-square-foot apartment in Israel. We would all have to rearrange our lives.

It was a long goodbye. For two years after they decided to make aliya, or move to Israel and become citizens, Marion and Joe Goodstein enjoyed farewell dinners and tributes to their half-century of service in the Knoxville, Tennessee, Jewish community. They rediscovered long-forgotten treasures tucked away in the recesses of their house. The closets and cupboards held Raggedy Ann and Andy dolls, toys, costumes and books from their married daughters' and son's childhood; newspaper clippings from Joe's heyday as a prominent architect; cookbooks from Marion's journey as wife, mother and grandmother to kosher caterer; and photos and heirlooms galore.

Relatives from across the United States and Israel came to help sift and sort the accumulation of a lifetime. Friends in the community offered packing assistance to close up the house at 520 Cherokee Boulevard that had seen not only a family reared, but also decades' worth of Sabbath dinners served, Passover seders hosted, and challas and Purim hamantaschen (pastry) baked and sold.

"We can't part with anything. We want to take it all," Marion laments months before the movers arrive. "We're downsizing from a six-bedroom house to a two-bedroom apartment," says Joe in the spacious old home place. "It will have a kitchen and a living/dining room combo. We're taking that couch, these two chairs, those two tables, those two breakfronts and folding chairs."

Both trusted that saying goodbye to many familiar faces and creature comforts would be worth the sacrifice. Although they were rooted in a large, longstanding circle of friends, they had no close family members left in Knoxville. Two of three children and 12 grandchildren lived in Israel. While the Goodsteins rarely had missed any recitals, graduations or skating competitions of two other grandchildren in Atlanta, Georgia, they barely ever had celebrated such milestones with the Israeli side of the family.

Marion remembers hearing of a children's book about a

boy who thought his grandparents lived on an airplane. Before moving to Israel, she related to the storyline. "That's the only way the grandkids ever see the grandparents. They go to the airport and meet them and take them back to the airport. We wanted a relationship with our grandkids in Israel."

The Goodsteins had traveled to Israel many times before they ever had grandchildren. Marion went for the first time in 1950 and dreamed of living there. But family ties pulled tightly at her heart, and the thought of separation was too painful. Her parents said to come back home and they would all travel to Israel together someday. They never did.

In those days, the trip from the Southern United States to Israel via connecting flights took 36 hours. Travelers didn't zip back and forth as they do now. Marion recalls the early days of the modern nation, when austerity reigned. Food, water, clothing and other necessities were rationed. As a student on a program, she counted herself lucky to have all she needed. Regular Israelis, on the other hand, had little.

Then the Korean War broke out. Israeli officials told Marion and other foreign students, "If you come home on the planes that we have allotted for you, we can get you home. If not, we cannot promise you any flight home." She took the ticket to America, and felt torn between two worlds for the next 56 years.

She and Joe traveled between the two worlds many times. They lost count after visiting Israel 50 or 60 times over the course of the years. The pull to the Holy Land included a daughter, Shari, and a son, David, who as adults had built families, lives and careers in Jerusalem. Another daughter, Fran, lived in Atlanta. Her two children knew their grandparents didn't live on a plane, because they often drove 200 miles down from Tennessee for recitals, graduations and other special occasions.

Marion and Joe knew that after making aliya at ages 77 and 80, they would be starting over. Their new identities would be reduced to Shari and David's mother and father or the 12 Israeli grandchildren's savta and saba – grandmother and grandfather.

"We're giving up a lifetime of relationships in Knoxville – relationships with family, the community, the synagogue. We're close to a dozen synagogues in our Jerusalem neighborhood. We'll find different ones and try different ones. But this one in Knoxville is mine, and I feel really attached to it. You give that up, and you don't replace that kind of a relationship," muses Marion during the process of their "long goodbye" to the United States.

"We have friends here. Hopefully, we'll have more friends there. Shari insists there are so many people our age in our Jerusalem neighborhood. We haven't met them yet. But here we have friends; some of them go back to when I came to school here in 1946. You don't replace 50-year friends with new friends. It doesn't work that way."

They had cast a wide net, hosting approximately 3,000 guests for meals on the Sabbath and Jewish festivals. Two widows were regulars for years; Joe graciously picked them up and drove them home. One, Dora Green, retained her humor and zest for life until she died at 103. When she went to synagogue, younger members would come up and talk to her because they knew her from the Goodsteins' Sabbath table.

Marion and Joe realized they would be giving up identities as leaders in the Knoxville Jewish community. She had served as president of the United Jewish Appeal-Federation, Hadassah and Sisterhood and as the first woman president of Heska Amuna Synagogue. She had supervised Heska Amuna's kosher kitchen, taught nursery school, and directed the Arnstein Jewish Community Center preschool. Joe's service positions had included chairmanship of the synagogue board, UJA-Federation and the Israel Bonds drive. "We used to say we played musical presidencies. People in a small town need to pitch in. There weren't many to take leadership roles," says Marion.

Known around town as the "challa lady," she operated Kosher Karry-outs, which sprouted up in 1982 when the World's

Fair brought Jews from far-flung cities to Knoxville. After the fair ended, Marion continued the business by baking goodies for the Sabbath, holidays and special events like bar and bat mitzva parties. Kosher Karry-outs was a labor of love for her, with the proceeds going to charity and paying for trips to Tennessee for her children and grandchildren in Israel.

Israel has plenty of challa ladies. Marion didn't worry about starting a business from scratch there. Instead, she anticipated taking Hebrew language immersion courses and unpacking all the boxes that would condense a lifetime into one lift shipped to Israel.

"From my point of view, we're gaining a relationship with the Jewish state, just like I always dreamed of. You don't have to think of what holiday it is. Every Jewish holiday, you don't have to stay out of school; it's a national holiday. You walk down the street and you have a flag of Israel. There's something about that. I've been involved, and my parents were very devout Zionists. I was raised in Young Judaea. I was raised thinking Israel was very much a part of my life. But to finally be able to live there and be a part of the state is a big thing for me."

Joe anticipated helping to shape the state, literally. An architect with a university basketball arena, 56 schools and many other landmarks to his credit in the United States, he looked forward to helping his daughter, Shari, in Israel. Also an architect, she had developed a loyal clientele, particularly in the Jewish Quarter of the Old City of Jerusalem, where civilizations are built on top of civilizations.

Before her parents' move to Israel, Shari renovated the apartment they bought as an investment in her neighborhood. The cozy new home would see many Sabbath and holiday guests; in Israel, they generally would be close relatives instead of the large adopted family Joe and Marion had created in Tennessee.

While their extended family in Knoxville would mourn their leaving, the time had come. As Marion says, "The ocean got wider and wider. Our kids started working on us for a long time, but we just weren't ready."

At last they were.

Davina Davidson

Alternative Therapist
Born 1959, Melbourne, Australia

Davina Davidson

$60, A Rucksack And God

It's erev Shabbat, Friday afternoon, as the Sabbath approaches. A chicken and casseroles are steaming in the oven. The salads are made. A bouquet of flowers and braided bread, challa, decorate a tiny kitchen in the Katamonim neighborhood of Jerusalem. The preparations finished, Davina Davidson retreats to her bedroom for our interview, closing out the sound of little ones playing in the adjacent living room. The door pops open once or twice, as the youngest children test their mother's boundaries during my visit.

Davina and her husband, Oded, an internationally known Judaica artist, have reared 10 children in this three-bedroom, one-bathroom apartment. Small quarters aside, I always marvel at how close the family is. Sure, they have their arguments, but in general, a feeling of love and warmth permeates their residence. It has been like a home away from home for me since we met in the mid-1990s, when I was studying Hebrew one summer in Israel.

Anative of Australia, Davina Davidson spent many lonely years as a girl in a Jewish children's home. Little did she dream that, as an adult, her life would be filled with a large, affectionate family – five boys and five girls. The sands shifted when Davina came to Israel as an 18-year-old university student one summer.

"It was a thorough tour of Israel from north to south. It was just before Sinai was given back," she recalls of the 10-week visit. "We even made it to Sharm el-Sheik. And from very close into the first few days even, I started to feel like, wow. It's really lovely to be among my own people. I started to think about staying."

She wrestled with whether or not to go back and finish her degree. In the end, the indescribable pull of Israel won out. Davina marvels at the chutzpa it took to stay: "I had $60 and one rucksack of clothes. And I knew nobody, because I had no relatives here. And I couldn't speak Hebrew.

"But I felt like this was where I needed to be. This was the place for me. I felt home, that feeling of, this is where I belong." Thousands of other immigrants to Israel from the four corners of the world understand that feeling.

In Australia, Davina never felt as if she belonged. As she says, it was like living "in somebody else's country." She and her siblings grew up with an Orthodox Jewish day school education. While she has no memories of overt anti-Semitism, "I never felt Australian. I always felt we were the Jews among the non-Jews."

The yearning to find her place was stirring. Davina didn't fit in any pigeonhole of the Jewish community whose customs she found too rigid.

"When I came to Israel, I just felt like there was so much more space as a Jew to be anything I wanted, not just a doctor or a lawyer or an accountant or a teacher. But I could search for me and still be among my people. And I loved the feeling of being able to talk about spiritual things and deeper things. I didn't have that experience so much in Australia."

As a teenager, she wore her otherness as an uncomfortable garment. When peers were chattering about Levi jeans and nail polish, Davina was worrying about children dying in Biafra. In Israel, however, she could communicate on a deep level with others and God.

The warm Mediterranean hospitality also fit her style. "People just opened their doors and collected you in," says the 40-something grandmother, whose home likewise is a crossroads for neighborhood children and friends.

A Yemenite family in Beersheba took her under their wing. The young Aussie met them while on the student tour, and they said she'd have a place to come if she decided to stay in Israel. She spent Sabbaths and holidays with her adopted clan, a white Australian among the dark Yemenites.

When Davina and Oded married, it was too far and expensive for her parents to travel to Israel, but the Yemenite friends stood in as family.

Davina began her life in the Holy Land cleaning people's houses, because she didn't need to speak Hebrew for that. "I could do that in the afternoon and study Hebrew in the morning."

Her love of children led to a job in a private kindergarten – where the little ones were her teacher. "That's where I got to practice Hebrew, talking to these 3- and 4-year-olds. We'd go for walks into the mountains outside of Jerusalem and pick flowers."

Meanwhile, for six months she bedded down on a couch in a student apartment. Later, upon visiting one of the old roommates there, she met Oded, who was a neighbor. There was an immediate bond. "This was the guy I could talk about anything with – music, philosophy, religion, science. We could also go out and have a raging good time, hiking, swimming, the beach, getting up at all hours of the day and night and going out on trips."

Often, the two would talk all night and then find

themselves walking to Damascus Gate and watching the Old City of Jerusalem wake up. "You could do that then; it wasn't dangerous," Davina reminisces. "There was a lovely little place we used to have tea and watch the Old City come alive. You could walk on the city walls."

They knew each other eight months before moving in together and marrying. Davina had dreamed of having many children – by Australian standards, five or six is a lot. "I'm sure Oded, being an only child, had no idea he was going to have 10 children."

The large number of children had nothing to do with being religious, which the Davidsons were after Oded started working as a freelance Judaica artist. Both felt uncomfortable about making Jewish ritual objects on the Sabbath, so he stopped working Saturdays. Then he started covering his head while he was working. They became more observant in stages.

"But now I would call us God-loving, more focused on the spiritual side and not so much on the law – even though we keep kosher and don't drive on Shabbat." She declares that her affinity for Israel has nothing to do with politics and everything to do with the presence of the Almighty: "I truly believe the hand of God is at work here. I live in Israel because this is the Holy Land."

After her fifth child was born, she dreamed that God's gift in this life was many children. The family struggled financially, but for years she wasn't too concerned. "That's just what happens when you have a big family," she reasoned.

"We lived very simply. The bare necessities. There were a lot of large families in Israel, and 15 or 20 years ago, it wasn't a purchasing culture. When I came to Israel, most people didn't have cars or televisions. We didn't look a lot different to the other people, although we would have looked very strange in Australia.

"We weren't theater-goers. We did things at home together: reading, artwork, music. I cooked simple food: rice, chicken, vegetables, a lot of salads. It was cheap food to feed huge quantities of people. I never bought lollies or junk food. There might not have been fruit every week, but there was clay to play with. There were crayons and pencils and paper for drawing. Oded would teach the kids to play chess. Or he would sit on the floor and show them how to build a silhouette theater."

When the two eldest, Liad and Naor, were babies, they would go to the park every day. Davina has fond memories of playing in the sand with them and making cakes, pretending. Ironically, nobody ever played games with her as a child. She has no memories of even being in a park.

"I loved reading stories to my kids. And I have no memories of ever being read to in the Jewish children's home. Many of them were children like myself whose parents were unable to take care of them. I wanted to do for my children what hadn't been done for me. My child inside also was getting nurtured."

Elchanan Davidson

Army
Born 1990, Jerusalem, Israel

Elchanan Davidson

Skateboard King With A Poet's Soul

The lanky boy flies five feet off the ground on his skateboard, arms spread like an eagle's wings for balance. Shirtless, black hair tucked in a ponytail, he looks intense while performing his latest athletic feat. The moment captured in time and space always gives me great joy whenever it flashes on my computer desktop. It makes me feel that I, too, could soar with the eagles. I could be fearless and rush head-on into new adventures. I could enjoy physical mastery, strength and grace.

I feel as proud of this teenager as if he were my own son. In fact, I consider Elchanan Davidson and his nine siblings, the children of my close friends in Jerusalem, as part of my extended family. They are always warm and loving, even though we see one another only every year or so. I relate to each one differently. Elchanan and I share a passion for writing, so that often dominates our conversations.

Tonight, which happens to be Halloween in the United States, we talk about everything from poetry to peace. It's a treat for me to hear about this young Israeli friend's life and dreams. Saturday night after *the conclusion of the Sabbath, on the back porch of his parents' home in the Katamonim section of town, we are bridging the gap between generations and cultures.*

Elchanan Davidson, a native Israeli, or Sabra, seemed to tumble out of the womb with energy to burn. His mother remembers him crawling at 5 months, walking at 10 months, climbing at 1 year and doing somersaults at 2 years after seeing an acrobatic circus.

At 7, he dove into the Jerusalem Circus, a group of teenagers and younger children from Israeli and Palestinian neighborhoods who trained and performed together for mixed audiences. He learned stilt walking, juggling and unicycle riding. Then at 9, Elchanan went to summer camp in America as part of Circus Smirkus, a nonprofit international youth circus where star-spangled skills range from clowning to tightrope walking.

Somewhere in the mix, Elchanan found time to act in a performing theater. As he recalls, "It was a place I could spread my energy around. It would make me calm. I was always running, jumping and climbing – even in class in school. You're really nervous at the start of the performance. You look at all the people. But when you get into it, it's a lot of adrenaline. You take your fear and perform, and you have a lot of confidence afterward."

As the sixth of 10 children born to Davina and Oded Davidson, he had a large audience just at home. In addition to his athletic prowess, the size of his family has drawn attention throughout Elchanan's life.

Born in 1990, he admits that sharing a three-bedroom, one-bath apartment with parents, brothers and sisters has presented challenges. "It's a lot of people in a little place, and you don't have your own space, and you have to share.

"But my brothers are my best friends. I go out with my brothers. I go camping with my brothers. I do everything with my brothers. They're my life. When I look at my friends who have four brothers or sisters in the family and everyone has their own space, their own computer, their own clothes – they don't go out together. They barely know each other. They go to their room, don't come out; they like their space, and they don't sit with their family.

"When they have a problem, they go to their parents or their friends. When I have a problem, I go to my brothers. They help me with anything. If I need money and I'm stuck somewhere in the Army, I call my brothers to send me money. They look out for me. Last night, when we all went out with my sister Michal and her boyfriend, she paid for me because I'm in the Army and didn't have money. That's what I call a family."

The married siblings remain close as well, coming home to share a Sabbath meal every two weeks. When he gets married, Elchanan wants his family to be like the one in which he grew up.

As many blessings as it brings, the large family has its limits, particularly in close confines. He acknowledges, "Even though it's great and amazing, if it's 10 o'clock at night and I want to write or play guitar, I can't. I have three brothers living in my room. They're asleep or they're studying. So I go out and write on a bench or something."

Elchanan balances his athletic gifts with artistic sensibilities. He started writing poems around age 14. His father had brought him five poetry books, which sparked the teenager's imagination.

"I started reading a lot. I have some in English, but most are in Hebrew. I started writing everything in my mind. I write about everything from love poetry and philosophy to heavy prose. It helps me express myself. I write things I wouldn't say to anyone. I write for myself. But if somebody read it, they would understand what they wanted to.

"I want to publish a book. My dream was to finish a book by the time I was 18. But it can't be anymore, because I'm 19. I started writing a book three months ago."

Growing up in a musical family, Elchanan also enjoys creative expression through guitar, piano and harmonica. His favorite performers cross different cultures, from Americans Neil Young, David Crosby and Paul Simon to Israelis Idan Raichel and Ha'Chaverim Shel Natasha (Friends of Natasha).

But this young man who has always had energy to burn can take sitting still for only so long. Elchanan counts skateboarding among his many passions. It all started when he received an Xbox with a skateboarding game as a bar mitzva present.

"I would skateboard every day. After school, I was going to the skate park every day. I miss those days," he says longingly. "It was almost the same as the circus. You have a trick and you stick to it and try it, try it and try it until you nail it.

"It's not scary. When you're in the air, it's fun. You always fall. Every day you skate, you fall, at least five times, 10 times. Me, I never broke anything. It's weird that it didn't happen."

Elchanan still likes to take his skateboard to the park with his buddies, but cannot do it every day now. He has obligations, such as Army service. He joined after high school at age 18. Due to recurring knee problems, he could not enlist as a combat soldier, so instead became a cook.

"Most of my jobs that I've worked in have been as a cook. I said if that's what I like to do, that's what I want to do in the Army. Everybody in my family knows how to cook. I think cooking is creative. There is stuff I learned from my family, stuff I made up, stuff I learned from my work. For instance, I fry cucumbers with soy sauce, balsamic vinegar and sugar and sprinkle sesame on top. You can eat it hot or cold."

Elchanan has been invited to take an Army officers' course, which would stretch his service in the military from three to four years. But he is game, because he wants to seize the opportunity to learn as much as possible.

He says growing up in Israel is hard because, "You finish school and you have to give three years to the Army. You start your life three years earlier in America – you go to college or university."

However, in certain ways, he believes he enjoys more freedom than young people in other countries. "My parents grew up in Brazil and Australia and said it wasn't safe to go out after 10 at night. Here, I can go out on the streets until 3 in the morning. You feel safe when you go out at night with your friends. When I was 5, I was going to kindergarten by myself. You have a lot of freedom."

That includes the freedom to date. The young philosopher muses, "I always say Jerusalem is a city of love. You can't just date here. Either you fall in love or she falls in love."

And, has he fallen in love? "Yes, a few times. Now I'm in the Army and focusing on the Army."

Yisrael Avidor

Born Jedrzejow, Poland
1926 – 2008

Yisrael Avidor

A Shepherd And A Diplomat

In all my trips to Israel, I'd never stayed at a kibbutz before, which is pretty amazing. Like Jaffa oranges and high-tech exports, kibbutzes have become symbols of the modern state. The first communal settlement sprouted up almost 40 years before the establishment of the State of Israel. In 1909, a group of young Jewish pioneers, mostly Eastern European, founded the Degania kibbutz south of the Sea of Galilee, which Israelis call Lake Kinneret. They were reclaiming the soil of their ancient homeland and sowing seeds for a new life.

My own imagination was fertile as a child. I pounded out the "Exodus" theme on our family piano in Tennessee, swaying to the passionate lyrics. "This land is mine, God gave this land to me." Movies, books and photos created exotic images of far-away Israel, including the tanned, rugged kibbutzniks.

And here I was, at last, meeting several on a visit to Kfar Hanassi. They included an Israeli with whom a matchmaker set me up! He kindly served as my guide.

Kfar Hanassi means "Village of the President" and honors Chaim Weitzman, Israel's first president. A granddaddy kibbutz founded in 1948 on a rise above the Jordan River, it lies 22 miles north of the Sea of Galilee, 30 miles south of the Lebanese border and two miles from the Golan Heights. Indeed, the place feels historic.

"See that woman over there? She was on the Exodus ship," a resident whispered to me in the dining hall. Also among the old-timers was Yisrael Avidor, who helped found the kibbutz – where he has lived since July 2, 1948 – and unexpectedly became a liaison to French President Francois Mitterrand.

Israel is a smorgasbord of cultures, and Yisrael Avidor blends several of them. A resident of Kibbutz Kfar Hanassi, he speaks different languages that reflect the chapters of his storied life.

Born in 1926 as Yisrael Breitbard, he didn't spend much of his childhood in his native Poland. At age 5, he moved with his family to the port town of Roanne on the Seine River in Normandy.

Thus, his Polish quickly gave way to French – which would come in handy one day in diplomatic relations with the president of France. But more about that later.

As Yisrael neared adulthood, a special teacher helped prepare him for his bar mitzva in January 1939 – a bittersweet time. Yisrael proudly sent a record of his bar mitzva speech back to relatives in Poland, where war flickered on the horizon. Violence erupted in September, when Germany invaded Poland and started World War II.

The following May, Germany attacked France. Yisrael spent the war years under Nazi occupation. At age 15, he volunteered through a youth scouts movement to hide Jewish children whose parents had been deported to concentration camps.

"My job was to find places where they could be adopted by families who sympathized with Jews and wouldn't give them over to the Germans. They were in a terrible position. They didn't know where their parents were," he recalls in an interview at the kibbutz nursing home.

Yisrael had a system. If he saw a Croix de Lorraine in the home, it meant the family was sympathetic to Jews. If he didn't notice a cross, the symbol of the Free French Forces under Charles de Gaulle, he quickly left.

He succeeded in finding homes for 33 youngsters. Many eventually made their way to Israel.

At some point, Yisrael believed he was being followed and could be in danger. His superiors immediately replaced his forged identity papers and got in touch with a priest named Father Victor Kolmer, who was principal of an agricultural boarding school in Nandax. Yisrael took refuge there when he was 17. Father Kolmer and another priest, Father Rene Delafosse, administrator of the school, were the only ones who knew Yisrael was Jewish. Several weeks later, the boy came down with rheumatic fever and one of his legs became paralyzed. Yisrael's parents came out of hiding to treat him, and he fully recovered. But then someone betrayed his parents to the Nazis. The couple were rounded up and sent to Auschwitz. They perished in the concentration camp.

In 1944, German soldiers raided the boarding school where Yisrael remained. As they examined pupils' identity papers, Yisrael kept his composure and claimed he was a devout Catholic – thereby maintaining his freedom. More than 50 years later, Yad Vashem, Israel's Holocaust Martyrs' and Heroes' Remembrance Authority, recognized the priests in its list of Righteous Among the Nations, rescuers of Jews during the Holocaust.

Before the war broke out, Yisrael recalls, his father, a right-wing Zionist, worked hard in a factory for a wealthy brother-in-law who seemed to exploit him. Yisrael's mother was a Labor Zionist who favored the creation of a Jewish state by working-class people building a society with rural kibbutzes.

Yisrael shared their dreams. Inspired by an Aliya Bet

representative who came to Roanne to talk to the Jewish community, the teenager volunteered for the clandestine immigration to Palestine.

The Hebrew word aliya means ascent and connotes immigration to the Land of Israel. Bet, the second letter of the Hebrew alphabet, implies something unofficial or secret. As the urgency for Jews to leave Europe intensified, Aliya Bet moved more than 100,000 refugees to Palestine, which was still under British control.

Jews had many plans to evade the strict British immigration quotas. Travel by ship became a main mode of transport, with the Mosad l'Aliya Bet, or Organization for Illegal Immigration, lighting the way.

Yisrael met Rachel, a spunky British woman with Habonim, a Zionist socialist youth movement, who was volunteering to get a Turkish boat for illegal immigrants ready to sail for Palestine. He and she had arrived the same evening at a camp sheltering the immigrants – Holocaust survivors from all over Europe.

The only French Rachel knew was, "I'm English. I don't speak French." The only English Yisrael knew was, "My tailor is rich. My tailor is poor." But between Hebrew, Yiddish and German, they managed to become acquainted over 13 days at sea on a boat headed to Palestine.

Their lives further overlapped when the British seized their boat, arrested the passengers and sent them to a detention camp in Cyprus for six months.

"Coming to Israel was difficult for us. We thought Israel would accept everybody. We saw that the British didn't want us to come so much. We had to fight two fronts. It also was hard starting here," Yisrael recalls.

He entered Palestine in 1946 at the age of 20. Fearing he was considered a deserter from the French army after he had fled the country with a Zionist socialist youth group, Yisrael changed his last name to Avidor. It means "father of the generations" in Hebrew.

Only later did he find out he was considered a war orphan, and had not been required to go into the French army after all.

Upon arrival in the land of their forefathers, Yisrael and Rachel had gone to another kibbutz in the Galilee. They were issued tents to live in on the banks of the Jordan.

Rachel recalls herself and Yisrael as a young pioneer couple with advanced ideas for those days. They saw no need to wait for an official ceremony, so they asked the kibbutz manager for a family tent.

The small round tent came with a metal bed frame and jute sack. "There's a bed, but where's the mattress?" they asked the kibbutz manager.

"Is there a sack on the bed?" he replied.

"Yes."

"Go to the cowshed and get straw to fill the sack. That's your mattress."

The young couple did exactly that, making the tent their home on Feb. 1, 1947. Then tradition won out. They decided to wed, and asked the kibbutz manager if a wedding allowance was in the budget. The kibbutz manager pulled a one-lira note from his pocket and announced, "That's plenty for a wedding."

"What about the ring?" asked Rachel. "Not in the budget," he responded.

After well-wishers loaned them a ring, Yisrael and his bride-to-be hitchhiked to Haifa, where immigrant friends threw a modest party for them. Then the couple made their vows under the chuppa, or wedding canopy, on March 17, 1947. The next day, they hitchhiked home to their tent on Kibbutz Kfar Blum, whose founding members mostly hailed from Britain, South Africa, the United States and Baltic countries.

The kibbutz had a carp farm where Yisrael worked initially. As he remembers, "It's very hard work, especially in the winter, when the water is like ice."

In 1948, Yisrael and Rachel helped found Kibbutz Kfar

Hanassi. There, he held widely varying jobs, from mayor to shepherd. "First of all, I was in charge of the socialist youth movement. I was secretary general. Afterwards, I became the person in charge of public relations of the Zionist youth movement Habonim. I got word to go back to France. Rachel and our daughter, Tsila, joined me."

As worldwide secretary, Yisrael worked for the Jewish Agency through Habonim.

Returning to the kibbutz, he held both high-profile and humble positions. He served as secretary, or mayor, of the little society. And he tended and milked sheep for four years.

Several among the 60 kibbutzniks often complained about the hardships. "Those who stayed with us stayed on our terms," says Yisrael.

Life may have been challenging, but it remained colorful. Yisrael remembers Col. Robert Henriques, a novelist and army officer from an old Jewish family in Britain, seeking to build a house at Kfar Hanassi.

"There was tremendous discussion on the kibbutz that a foreigner was Reform. The Reform movement sent a letter that we should make room for him and his dog. We decided he could build a house here. And when he died, the house would go back to the kibbutz."

That was one of the richest periods in Yisrael's memory at Kibbutz Kfar Hanassi.

In the 1970s, he sparked a French connection. Jean-Christophe Mitterrand, the son of the future president of France, was having a difficult time in his life and thought a kibbutz might be healing. Thus, the young man arrived for a stint at Kfar Hanassi.

"He worked everywhere, made a lot of friends, and we got very friendly. His mother, Danielle, used to come to see her son on the kibbutz. She stayed with us for a few weeks. I remember playing French Scrabble with her. We had a marvelous time together, and we got very friendly."

The families began a tradition of exchanging holiday greeting cards. "I send her religiously a luach (Jewish calendar) every year."

Because of Yisrael's ongoing relationship with the family, Israeli Prime Minister Shimon Peres asked him to serve as an envoy to Francois Mitterrand, by then president of France.

Yisrael accepted the offer, and tapped Mitterrand for support in various arenas. "I used to buy patisseries and bring them for breakfast, and he said, 'Yes Mr. Avidor, what have you got to sell me today?' Like this, I established a contact which was very important for the politics of Israel."

For example, Israelis wanted France's help to persuade Russian authorities to free Soviet Jews.

"That was a very important job," Yisrael states with pride. The influence helped Vladimir Slepak, Natan Sharansky and other famous "refuseniks," Jews whom the Soviet Union refused to allow to leave, to move to Israel at last.

The French connection became part of Israel's history. So has Yisrael. The shepherd-turned-diplomat continues to work four hours a day on the kibbutz he helped found in 1948. He packs cigarettes and chocolates for the communal store to sell.

By helping the kibbutz, he, in turn, is helped. "First of all, it gives you an occupation. This is important any time of life, and especially in old age. The fact that you do it together with other people, it gives you a feeling of continuity."

Yisrael and Rachel own their house on the kibbutz, where 30 family members live, including children, in-laws and grandchildren. In addition, they have an extended family of friends. Yisrael describes the community as loving and close.

"We are still so small. We have about 220 friends here. Most youngsters are not staying with their parents on the kibbutz anymore. The old generation is in charge of everything. All the kibbutzes are in a big dilemma," as younger generations move away.

But for Yisrael, who endured black scorpions, hornets, tent living and outdoor toilets in his pioneer days, "I wouldn't live anywhere else. I feel like this place gave me so much. I owe it my past, present and future."

Shlomo Molla

Knesset Member, Kadima Party
Born 1965, Macha, Ethiopia

Shlomo Molla

Walking Out Of Ethiopia

I know from experience that making aliya, or becoming an Israeli citizen, can be a lovely dream but a hard reality. Wrestling with the decision, financing it, doing the paperwork and juggling logistics are only the beginning. The cultural adjustments to life in Israel can prove unexpected and challenging.

I moved with two dogs to Jerusalem before the existence of Nefesh B' Nefesh, the organization that softens the way for North American and British immigrants. Nefesh helps with everything from planning to job-hunting to emotional support. New citizens on Nefesh flights landing at Ben-Gurion Airport receive the red carpet treatment, with politicians, photographers and flags greeting them.

For someone like me who arrived anonymously on El Al, it's hard to observe all the ceremony and not feel envious.

Then I meet Shlomo Molla and marvel at the even wider gulf his story entails. Leaving behind his family in Gondar Province at age 16, he and a group of boys walked 780 kilometers, or 485 miles, across Ethiopia

*and Sudan to achieve the dream of living in Israel.
Rescued by special operatives from the Israeli Mossad,
the national intelligence agency, they arrived in the
Holy Land via an airlift on Hercules transport planes.
No one padded their landing, but that didn't matter.
They were home.*

It's a blustery, rainy day in Tel-Aviv. Schools are closed in
Jerusalem because of snow. Shlomo Molla, bundled in a
white sweater, is reminiscing about his arrival in Israel
in February 1984. Many aspects of life in the Jewish homeland
caught him by surprise. "It was very cold like today. In Ethiopia,
it's very sunny.

"The second thing was all the people around me were white
people. I didn't understand that."

Coming from Gondar Province of Ethiopia, where his father,
Zemene, grew crops and tended cows and sheep, Shlomo felt
overwhelmed by the buildings and technology. He was confused
seeing Jews in Israel using cars on the holy Sabbath instead of
walking.

In Macha, his small tropical Ethiopian village, the 300
Jewish families practiced their religion without the influences
of modernity. They observed customs as Jews had in the First
Temple period, 1006 to 586 B.C.E.

Isolated, without any connection to Jews around the world,
the villagers learned their traditions orally from rabbis. Everyone
10 and older studied Judaism three hours a day until they were
married, he says.

However, they could not learn Hebrew or practice Judaism
in public after the Communist regime took over in 1973. Jews
were second-class citizens. Ethiopia's constitution prohibited
them from owning land. As Shlomo observes, "It's very difficult
to survive if you don't own your own land. My father, a farmer,
was bringing home one-third of his product; the rest went to

the government."

Villagers didn't mix with residents of other Ethiopian villages. "We lived a typical African village life. He and my mother didn't know how to read and write. It was an agricultural life. We had no electricity, no clinic, no bank, no public school in every village, no transportation," Shlomo says, sitting in an office at the Jewish Agency, or Sochnut, where he works. It's hard not to notice the cell phone and laptop with wireless mouse next to him.

In Ethiopia, he walked nine miles to and from his Jewish high school.

Shlomo's mother, Trunesh, has no formal education, but he speaks with pride and respect for her wisdom. It is a knowledge born of life experience. Trunesh had her first son at age 14. It's not unusual for Ethiopian girls to marry at age 12 and boys at 15 or 16.

"Here in Israel or in Western countries, there is a boyfriend and girlfriend," muses Shlomo, who was called Neguse, which means "king," in his native country. "In Ethiopia, they are not going to be lawyers or doctors, but are going to build an agricultural life."

Instead of marrying at age 16, Shlomo was trekking 780 kilometers, or 485 miles, across Ethiopia and Sudan with 15 friends from his native Gondar Province. He had grown up with a Zionist ideology and was trying to reach Israel.

"We believed Israel was the Promised Land, a homeland for all the Jews in the Diaspora (dispersion throughout the world). All the Jews have to come home to build Israel."

Shlomo grabbed his chance. Word had it that Israeli intelligence operatives from the Mossad were working in Sudan to rescue Ethiopians.

"We grew up with the story of Exodus, how Moshe got others to walk to Israel. It's a mitzva. We weren't naive. We'd be crossing the jungle and the desert. But we decided to take a chance."

The dangerous terrain was only one of many hurdles. Shlomo faced a difficult choice about whether or not to separate from his family. In the end, he left behind his parents, two sisters and nine brothers.

He was familiar with Genesis, which says, "Lech lecha. Go out of thy land, and from thy kindred, and from thy father's house, unto the land that I will show thee. And I will make of thee a great nation, and I will bless thee."

So Shlomo went out of his land, from his family and his father's house. Ethiopian Jews had dreamed of going to Israel since the modern nation's birth in 1948. They heralded Israel as their true homeland.

His band of boys hired a Christian guide to lead the way out. In the jungle, they encountered lions and tigers. But Shlomo and his friends took that part of the adventure in stride. "As Africans, it wasn't a big deal," he declares. "We knew how to protect ourselves."

But then robbers captured the lot, taking the boys' food, clothing and money. As prey to wild men, the young Jews felt themselves to be in great danger.

But the boys didn't have guns, and that worked to their advantage. Unarmed, they said they were refugees, and the robbers let them go.

Life in the desert was brutal. Shlomo and his friends had no water, food or shade. After one week, they were captured by Sudanese police, who shot and killed one of the boys. The police jailed the rest for 91 days, torturing and beating the Ethiopian youths, who didn't have any documents on them.

Then, surprisingly, the officers gave the boys their freedom, driving them by truck to a refugee camp. Shlomo had never ridden in a vehicle before. In the camp, for only the second time in his life, he met white people.

One of them, dressed in Arab garb, said mysteriously, "I know where you're coming from. What village." He met the boys later and ordered them to follow him. Apprehensively, they did so and saw groups of people climbing into trucks. They drove through the Sudan desert in the middle of the night to a military airport near Khartoum.

"We thought they would deport us to a neighboring country. We didn't know who they were," says Shlomo. The secretive "Arab" man gave a sign, and suddenly parachutists rained from the sky. An airplane landed noiselessly.

"Baruchim habaim (welcome). We're Israelis," said the white men.

The 420 Ethiopian Jews started crying, clapping and singing "Shalom Aleichem." Under a shroud of secrecy, they were airlifted to Israel. After a four-hour flight that capped many years of waiting, they had come to the Promised Land in "Operation Moses."

Shlomo remembers the day clearly: Feb. 1, 1984. Tirza, a 12-year-old girl who would become his wife, arrived from Ethiopia the same year. He would have to wait seven years to see his parents and siblings again.

In some ways, the attainment of Israel proved anticlimactic after Shlomo's 3 1/2-month journey, most of it spent in jail. He says pointedly, "My dream was to see milk and honey, something special, in Jerusalem. Reality was the Western Wall, some stones. That's it. In some ways, it was disappointing."

At first, he lived in an absorption center in the holy city of Tsfat, also known as Safed, high in the mountains of the Upper Galilee. Like other young new immigrants, Shlomo, a native Amharic speaker, took a crash course in Hebrew at an ulpan, or immersion program.

Then the teenage boy became a student at the prestigious Leo Baeck High School on Haifa's Mount Carmel. He flourished in the middle-class Israeli environment, so different from his rural, mostly undeveloped province.

"I'm very happy I chose to go to that school, because it gave me the basis of my life," Shlomo asserts. "Rabbi Samuel, a Reform rabbi, was a special person. He was my psychologist; he was my father; he was my brother; he was my teacher."

As Shlomo says, he had found a surrogate father. The young man was separated from his family of origin until 1991, when a covert Israeli airlift rescued his parents and 10 siblings, along with more than 14,000 other Ethiopian Jews.

Under "Operation Solomon," named for the king from whom Ethiopian Jews may be descended, the Israeli government authorized a special permit for its airline, El Al, to fly on the Sabbath. Beginning Friday, May 24, and continuing nonstop for 36 hours, 34 El Al jumbo jets and Hercules C-130s – with seats removed to fit in more people – whisked the Jews from Ethiopia to Israel.

Shlomo hadn't been in touch with his family for many years. Because Ethiopia was under Communist rule, letters from the democracy of Israel weren't allowed.

His parents and siblings had attempted an escape after Shlomo left on his trek across Ethiopia and Sudan, but they saw the trip was too dangerous. Ayele, his 9-year-old brother, had died in the desert – possibly due to lack of water.

By the time the family reunited, Shlomo had overcome culture shock and was well-integrated into Israeli society. He served as a military officer, graduated from Bar Ilan University's School of Social Work and obtained a second degree – an LLB, or bachelor of laws.

He went on to head Ethiopian Immigration and Absorption for the Jewish Agency, using his own experience to help ease the way for fellow countrymen who had endured difficult journeys.

"First of all, I'm an Israeli," Shlomo says proudly. "As an Israeli and a Jew, it's so special to understand the Ethiopian Jewish background."

He brings a new image of what it means to be Israeli to those he meets in his current job as head of the Jewish Agency's Zionist Activity in Israel Department. Shlomo represents one face of Israel to organizations like the United Nations, American

Jewish Congress, World Jewish Congress, American Israel Public Affairs Committee and United Jewish Communities.

"We came in at this very special time to be a bridge," Shlomo says, referring to the Ethiopian Jewish community.

"Theodor Herzl (founder of modern Zionism) was thinking and talking about black Jews. Black Ethiopian Jews didn't think there were white Jews. White Jews didn't think there were black Jews. There were two parallel assumptions."

In Ethiopia, he didn't know from Reform, Conservative, Orthodox or secular. As he says, "You are a Jew; you're born a Jew; you practice Judaism."

Families in his native land were strictly observant in pre-Talmudic Jewish traditions. The women went to the mikva, or ritual bath, and Ethiopian Jews continued to carry out ancient festivals such as Seged that have been passed down generation to generation.

They had lost contact with the Western world more than a century before the Talmud's completion.

That's why they were offended when some Israeli rabbis claimed the Ethiopians were descended from the Tribe of Dan – but wanted to convert them anyway to make sure they were authentically Jewish. As Shlomo says, "For us, it felt so bad. You come and tell me I'm not a pure Jew. How can you judge me? We do brit mila (circumcisions), Passover, everything. We do the mitzvot, the korban Pesach (the sacrifice of Passover also known as the paschal lamb)."

Ovadia Yossef, Israel's chief Sephardic rabbi, said in 1972, "I have come to the conclusion that Falashas (Ethiopian Jews) are Jews who must be saved from absorption and assimilation. We are obliged to speed up their immigration to Israel and educate them in the spirit of the holy Torah, making them partners in the building of the Holy Land."

Shlomo and his family have helped build the society. His wife teaches science at the Weizmann Institute, and they have two daughters and a son.

"We're not doing badly in Israel," Shlomo says, matter of factly.

His dream was to strengthen the connection between Diaspora Jews and Israel. "I want to build more of a bridge." Soon after the interview, he was elected to the Israeli Knesset, or parliament, and realized the opportunity he had begun to create as a youth with his journey across the desert.

About the Photographer

Born in Johannesburg, South Africa, David Silverman moved to Israel in 1983, enrolled in the Camera Obscura visual arts college and studied photography in Jerusalem and Tel-Aviv. He began his career as a news photographer in Israel in 1991. Working first for Reuters and then for Getty Images, he has photographed the Israeli-Palestinian conflict, the three monotheistic religions and their annual festivities, regional politics and daily life. He has traveled to neighboring countries and beyond, covering news and feature stories. His photos have appeared in books, major newspapers and newsmagazines across the world.

David took all the photographs in this book except for the following:

- Ronda Robinson (photo by Steven Bridges)
- Marion and Joe Goodstein (photo by Lloyd Wolf)
- Miri Flusser (photo by Ronda Robinson)
- Shlomo Molla (photo courtesy of Knesset Member Shlomo Molla's office)

CPSIA information can be obtained at www.ICGtesting.com
Printed in the USA
LVOW090712020612

284361LV00003B/3/P